Subaru Impreza Group A Rally Car

1993 to 2008 (includes all rally cars)

First published in October 2017

A catalogue record for this book is available from the British Library.

ISBN 978 1 78521 110 2

Library of Congress control no. 2017933526

Published by Haynes Publishing,
Sparkford, Yeovil,
Somerset BA22 7JJ, UK.
Tel: 01963 440635
Int. tel: +44 1963 440635
Website: www.haynes.com

Haynes North America Inc.,
859 Lawrence Drive, Newbury Park,
California 91320, USA.

Printed in Malaysia.

Subaru Impreza Group A Rally Car

1993 to 2008 (includes all rally cars)

Owners' Workshop Manual

An insight into the design, engineering and competition history of Subaru's iconic rally car

Andrew van de Burgt

Contents

OPPOSITE **The stunning vistas of New Zealand were fertile grounds for the Impreza. Colin McRae is seen here in 1994.** *(Prodrive)*

RIGHT **This book will take you under the skin of one of the most iconic rally cars.** *(Adam Warner)*

Introduction

The Subaru Impreza, perhaps more than any other race or rally car, transformed the image of the brand and helped to prove that the old motorsport adage of 'win on Sunday, sell on Monday' still had some truth to it.

In the hands of drivers such as Colin McRae, Richard Burns and Petter Solberg, the blue and gold Impreza rally cars became famous the world over and created a legion of fans who to this day still gather in their thousands to celebrate these incredible machines.

This book tells the story of how the relationship between Subaru and Prodrive was born, how the demands of the stages shaped the design and development of the car and the processes involved in keeping one of the 63 Group A versions of the Impreza that were originally built competitively active today. I have spoken to many of those involved on the original rally programme, as well as the drivers and co-drivers themselves, with the hope of creating a complete and definitive guide to this most iconic car.

The book also looks at the legacy of the Group A car and how the lessons learned in its development informed the design of the World Rally Car version that succeeded it and upheld the Impreza's incredible record of success.

Finally, I look at the cars the Impreza had to beat in order to claim the title of World Champion. In an era of rallying heavyweight marques such as Lancia, Toyota and Ford, the story of how a comparatively unknown brand like Subaru was able to take on and beat the best makes for compelling reading.

Acknowledgements

The many people and organisations that have helped me with this project in many different ways include: David Richards; David Lapworth; Anthony Peacock; David Evans; Ryan Champion; Ian Gwynne; Ari Vatanen; Fabrizio Brivio; Pete Collen; World Rally Archive; eWRC-results; Robert Reid; Ben Sayer; Sam Smith; Kevin Wood; LAT Archive; Ben Anderson; Carlos Sainz; Markku Alen; Ian Moreton; Scott McBurney; Tony Hawtin; Tony Sircombe; Pierro Liatti; and Adam Warner. I thank them all.

OPPOSITE Sainz kicks up the gravel as he powers on in Portugal in 1994. *(Prodrive)*

Chapter One

The Subaru Impreza story

From obscure maker of minicars to standing at the top of the World Rally Championship, Subaru's rise is one of the great motorsport stories. None of this would have been possible without the hard-work, inspiration and dedication of the teams from Prodrive in the UK and STi in Japan. It wasn't always an harmonious relationship, but the results provided the proof that there was magic in the mixture.

OPPOSITE Perhaps the defining moment in Impreza history – McRae in action during the 1995 Rally GB. *(Prodrive)*

The birth of Subaru

The Subaru car company dates back to 1958, when it was established by Fuji Heavy Industries (FHI), although a prototype bearing the same name – and the seven sisters' constellation badge – was initially built in 1954. That first car was the 360, a 16bhp minicar that was nicknamed the 'Ladybug' in Japan and was built through to 1971. Featuring a tiny 356cc two-cylinder engine, a small number were exported to the United States. Despite its small size and low power, it had some racing pedigree in the T-1 class of the domestic Japanese saloon car championship.

It wasn't until the development of the next model, the four-door, front-wheel-drive Subaru 1000, that the cars were officially made available in Europe in the mid-1960s. But the really significant thing about the 1000 was that it featured a flat-four 'boxer' engine, a type with which the Subaru name is still synonymous today.

The next all-new model from the company was the Leone in 1971, the line-up for which included a four-wheel-drive estate version. This was a groundbreaking development for a mass-market affordable road car and would be the foundation of Subaru's first serious foray into the world of motorsport.

Subaru enters rallying

Subaru first hit the World Rally Championship stages in 1980, when a pair of hatchback versions of the 4x4 Leone (registered simply as 'Subaru Hatchbacks') were entered in the gruelling Safari Rally in the G1 class. By finishing 18th overall, Takeshi Hirabayashi and co-driver Aslam Khan claimed the class win.

Subaru returned to the Safari in 1983 with a four-car line-up that featured race and rally legend 'Quick' Vic Elford, a pair of Japanese drivers – Yoshinobu Takahashi and Yoshio Takaoka – and local hotshoe Frank Tundo. Takaoka and co-driver Shigeo Sunahara finished an impressive fifth to claim class honours once more, while Takahashi came home seventh. The remaining two cars retired.

The inaugural New Zealand Rally took place later that year. On the entry list was a Subaru 4WD (it was a Leone RX) from Motor Holdings Ltd. Its driver, Kiwi Peter 'Possum' Bourne, finished 14th, but first in Group A, and the start of a long and successful relationship with the marque had begun.

For 1984 Subaru entered a car for Shekhar Mehta on the Monte Carlo Rally as well as one for team regular Takaoka. Mehta took 14th overall, fifth in class, while Takaoka was a distant 35th. It was the marque's first rally in Europe, but its programme remained low-key, with further outings in the Safari and with Bourne in New Zealand its only real activity outside of Japan.

Following the introduction of a new RX Turbo in 1985, a more expanded programme was introduced for 1986 and class honours duly followed once again on the Safari, as Mike Kirkland and Tundo finished fifth and sixth overall. It also featured the first excursion in the US, where Bourne took eighth place, and second in class, on the first ever Olympus Rally.

The programme was scaled up even further for 1987 as WRC rally winner Per Eklund joined the team and finished 12th on his debut in Monte Carlo. He was joined in the line-up by 1981 World Champion Ari Vatanen as part of a four-car assault on the Safari later that year. Eklund was fifth, while Vatanen was tenth, one place ahead of Bourne, which was enough to scoop the Team prize. It would be the Kiwi who secured Subaru's first WRC podium, when he came home third in that year's Rally New Zealand.

In 1988 FHI created Subaru Technical International (STi), which would act as its motorsport and high-performance tuning division. The two men put in charge of this project were Noriyuki Koseki and Ryuichiro Kuze, who would have a profound effect on the destiny of Subaru's rally programme.

One of the first things they did was make contact with British race and rally preparation specialists Prodrive, as the company founder and CEO David Richards recalls: 'We were running the BMW M3s in those days, and Mr Kuze, who was a sort of semi-retired chap from Subaru, came to the 1000 Lakes Rally,' he says. 'He was running STi – the sports arm – and he'd been given the task of looking at a motorsport programme with the idea of using it to lower the age profile of their customers, which was clearly a problem for them, and they were anticipating the introduction of the Impreza about two years later.

'I met him in Finland in 1988 and again in 1989. In April after the Safari Rally he contacted me and asked if he could visit me in England. So he came over to see us here and said, "Look, we want to build a car for the World Rally Championship, I've seen what you do on the BMWs and I'm very impressed with that. Would you be interested in working with us?" So we prepared a presentation for him and by the time he was back in Japan it was sitting on his desk ready to go.'

The presentation clearly had its desired impact, and in September 1989 it was confirmed that Prodrive would be preparing the new Legacy model for a full works entry into the WRC.

'An exciting combination enters the World Rally Championship in 1990,' the press release read. 'Subaru and Prodrive. Subaru have a long established reputation for producing the World's leading four wheel drive road cars. The Prodrive pedigree has been built on success: providing high quality; high performance, engineering solutions that get results. The Subaru Legacy Group A Rally Car – a joint venture of engineering excellence.'

Prodrive's test team manager Ian Moreton collected the first Legacy RS from the airport and, together with technical director David Lapworth, set about assessing the potential of their new project. 'It was quite a big car, but

rallying was slightly different then,' he says. 'You had plenty of space, so you weren't constrained by putting the spare wheel in and you could be quite liberal with how you laid everything out as long as you stayed inside the wheel base. You weren't battling for space all the time. But it had good suspension travel and we could get the right-sized wheels in there without having to do too much cutting and shutting to the bodywork.'

The official homologation for the Legacy arrived in January 1990 and the first of the Prodrive-built cars made their WRC debut on the Safari Rally. Rally legend Markku Alen was brought on board to lead the driver line-up and was supported by Bourne, Kirkland and local ace Ian Duncan, who'd taken sixth place for Subaru back in the 1988 running of the event.

ABOVE David Richards (centre) masterminded the Prodrive/Subaru relationship. *(LAT)*

BELOW Subaru's early rally activities centred around the Safari. The sixth-placed Jim Heather-Hayes/Anton Levitan Legacy RS is seen here in 1990. *(LAT)*

ABOVE **The ill-fated, short-lived Subaru F1 programme was a total failure. The Coloni-Subaru of Bertrand Gachot sits in the garage at the 1990 US Grand Prix prior to an attempt at pre-qualifying.** *(LAT)*

Alen got off to a flying start, and was leading the rally when a build-up of mud on the radiator caused the engine to overheat. More engine problems blighted Alen next time out in the Acropolis Rally, but he made the finish to record a solid fourth in his home event – the 1000 Lakes Rally. The Finn once again showed the potential of the car by leading in the early stages of the season finale, Rally GB. However, once again he was hobbled by engine issues, this time a blown turbo.

The WRC wasn't Subaru's only motorsport project in 1990. In 1989 it contracted Italian engine builder Motori Moderni to make them a 3.5-litre, flat-12 engine, which would be used by the tiny Coloni Formula 1 team the following season. Dubbed the Subaru 1235, the engine hit the test track at the end of 1989. While its design offered some theoretical aerodynamic benefits, in reality the engine was overweight and underpowered – an unholy combination in motorsport – so it was no surprise when Bertrand Gachot was slowest of all on the car's debut in Phoenix pre-qualifying.

Eight races and eight failures to pre-qualify later, and the project was canned. Coloni reverted to the Cosworth DFV, and Subaru's very brief and ill-fated Formula 1 project was over. Luckily, things were going rather better on the rally stages…

Alen kicked off his 1991 season with a podium finish in Sweden (the team skipped Monte Carlo), and backed this up with fifth next time out in Portugal, where teammate François Chatriot was sixth.

Duncan was sixth on the Safari, Chatriot ninth in Corsica, but Alen crashed out of the Acropolis. He bounced back with fourth in New Zealand, although engine issues accounted for Bourne. The team didn't enter Rally Argentina, but when it returned for the 1000 Lakes so did the engine issues, which caused Alen to retire. However, he did set five fastest stage times and led the rally during the opening leg.

Alen was back in the points with fourth in Australia, but the team stayed away from the rallies in San Remo, Ivory Coast and Spain. Alen was then part of a three-car assault on Rally GB, with Vatanen rejoining the fold and Colin McRae handed a Subaru WRC debut.

Alongside the World Rally programme, Prodrive had also been running the Group A Legacy RS in the British Rally Championship, and the young Scot had dominated the championship, earning his call-up to the WRC squad. McRae showed his potential by setting seven fastest stage times and was leading the event after Special Stages 12 and 13 before he eventually crashed out. Alen also led before

crashing out, which left Vatanen to salvage a result for the team with fifth place.

McRae retained his BRC title in style for Subaru in 1992 and was given five WRC outings alongside this as teammate to Vatanen. McRae was a fine second in Sweden, scoring Subaru's best WRC result to date. He starred on the Acropolis too, setting 11 fastest stage times on his way to fourth place. However, all three cars – Bourne had joined Vatanen and McRae – suffered engine

RIGHT McRae's second place in the 1992 Rally Sweden was the Legacy's best result so far. *(LAT)*

BELOW McRae won the 1992 BRC in a Prodrive-run Legacy. *(LAT)*

problems in New Zealand, though both cars made the finish in Finland, with Vatanen fourth and McRae eighth.

It was in 1992 that STi launched its first road car, a rally-inspired version of the Legacy. Over the years there would be a series of these low-volume, high-performance models created, all with significant input from Prodrive as they helped the homologation procedure required by the rules. But they would also become highly desirable and collectable models that were key in establishing Subaru as a cool and credible road car manufacturer for arguably the first time in its history.

Back on the stages, McRae was in inspired form in Rally GB, setting eight fastest stage times – more than anyone else in the event – only for technical issues to limit him to sixth. Vatanen was second, and with the new Impreza model having been launched in Japan things were looking rosy for 1993.

However, the new car wouldn't be ready until mid-season, and Subaru didn't want to make the old car redundant until it had a win to its name, so the Legacy still had a duty to perform. McRae was third in Sweden, and Vatanen was leading in Greece when he crashed out, but it all came together for McRae in New Zealand, where he drove brilliantly to secure his and Subaru's first rally win. It was

enough for him to claim fifth in the drivers' championship and help Subaru to third in the manufacturers' standings.

From humble beginnings, the Japanese marque was now a world-beater. On top of this Richard Burns had taken over from McRae in the BRC and claimed that title as well, while elsewhere Bourne wrapped up the Asia-Pacific Rally Championship in his Prodrive-built Legacy RS. On top of all this the Impreza would perform brilliantly on its WRC debut, with Vatanen challenging for the win on the 1000 Lakes. Exciting times indeed for all involved back at STi.

'They were a little company in Japan,' recalls David Richards. 'Mr Kuze was an exceptional individual and he and I had a very special relationship. I don't think they ever really believed that they could punch above their weight so much – they were always the little ones against Ford Motor Company, Toyota, Lancia etc. But it didn't happen overnight. The

ABOVE McRae scored more WRC points as he took sixth in the 1992 RAC Rally. *(LAT)*

LEFT Richard Burns took over from McRae as Subaru's lead BRC driver for 1993. *(LAT)*

15

BELOW David Richards was the 1981 World Champion co-driver alongside Ari Vatanen. *(LAT)*

BOTTOM Prodrive's first programmes were with Porsche in the European Rally Championship. Henri Toivonen in spectacular form on the 1984 Rally Ypres *(LAT)*

first year was 1990 with Alen, and we had a lot of engine issues, so we took the engine in-house. We took a while to sort the engine out – it took a year or two. We learnt a lot with the Legacy. We got the reliability then, and when the Impreza came on the scene it was clear it was a different kettle of fish altogether.'

There was another big change that happened in 1993: the introduction of cigarette sponsor 555 and its royal blue and gold livery. It would become a look that defined a generation of road car imitations too. Prodrive had brokered the agreement with British American Tobacco, which further strengthened its hand in the relationship.

'Because they had no infrastructure there as such they did give us a big free hand, and we'd also found BAT as a sponsor with 555, so that would have been paying more than half the budget,' says Richards. 'So with that in mind we were very much doing our own thing from here. We helped with the marketing – we were dealing with the dealers, all the livery, the clothing, every aspect of the team we were operating from here, so it really was a full turn-key solution.

'If I look back at the history of the company I would say that was the most significant programme we ever did. It's easy to forget now how high-profile it was at the time. It wasn't back pages of newspapers, it was front pages. And with Colin McRae, followed by Richard Burns, the following we had in Britain was just extraordinary!'

Prodrive

Prodrive was founded by David Richards and Ian Parry in 1984. Richards began rally co-driving in the early seventies while at the same time studying chartered accountancy. His big break in co-driving came when he was contracted by British Leyland to partner Tony Pond in 1976, but it was Ari Vatanen with whom he enjoyed his greatest success, winning the 1981 World Championship in a Ford Escort 1800T.

Alongside his co-driving Richards had already started out in business, establishing a motorsport consultancy with strong links to the Middle East. It was only natural, then, that Prodrive's first event was the 1984 Qatar International Rally, which it duly won with a Porsche 911 SC RS. With backing from Rothmans, Prodrive went on to win the 1984 Middle East Rally Championship, while with Henri Toivonen at the wheel its 911 also took runner-up honours in the European Rally Championship.

The programme expanded to include running a Metro 6R4 in the British and Irish championships in 1986 for Jimmy McRae, while a year later Prodrive began a relationship with BMW that yielded its first WRC win – on the 1987 Tour de Corse with Bernard Beguin – and would also take them into the world of circuit racing. Prodrive-built BMW M3s would dominate the British Touring Car Championship in the late 1980s, winning the title in 1988, 1989 and 1990.

The success of Prodrive's BMW programme

LEFT Prodrive ran Jimmy McRae in the BRC in a Metro 6R4 during 1986. *(LAT)*

attracted the attention of Subaru and led to a relationship that lasted from 1990 to 2008. It is one that was revived for a storming lap-record attempt of the Isle of Man TT course with a WRX STi and Mark Higgins in 2016.

In the intervening years Prodrive has expanded into a truly global operation, running projects in everything from Le Mans to V8 Supercars and World Rallycross. But that's only a fraction of the business, as its Advanced Technology arm – which takes the high-tech, precision engineering expertise gathered in motorsport and applies it across a wide array of other disciplines, including composites and electric powertrains – now accounts for roughly 50% of its turnover.

From its beginnings at Silverstone, Prodrive now has a state-of-the-art facility in Banbury, where, of course, a Group A Impreza takes pride of place in the reception area. Richards

CENTRE Bernard Beguin scored Prodrive's first WRC win in Corisca 1987 in a BMW M3. *(LAT)*

RIGHT Prodrive also ran BMWs in the BTCC, taking class honours with Frank Sytner. Sytner is seen here at Brands Hatch in 1988. *(LAT)*

was awarded a CBE for his services to the British motorsport industry in the 2005 New Year's Honours list.

The Group A regulations

Prodrive built the Legacy and the original Impreza to Group A (A8) regulations, as defined by motorsport's governing body the Fédération Internationale d'Automobile (FIA). Group A regulations had been introduced by the FIA, which was known as FISA (Fédération Internationale du Sport Automobile) at the time, at the start of 1982 as a replacement for Group 2, which was a category for modified touring cars.

The first series to embrace the new rules was the European Touring Car Championship, with domestic series in Britain, Germany, Australia and Japan soon following suit. This led to the creation of cars such as the Rover Vitesse, BMW 635i, Volvo 240 and – probably most famous of all – the Ford Sierra RS500 and Nissan Skyline GT-R (R32).

While Group A cars were entered in the World Rally Championship (including those from Subaru in the early days) the top class of cars was Group B, a category for flame-spitting, turbocharged and supercharged bespoke (200 road-going models were supposed to be created) stage monsters, which was also introduced in 1982 as a replacement for the Group 4 and 5 categories.

The governing body had intended to

supersede Group B with Group S in 1988. Speaking in the 1980s, FISA technical commission president Gabriel Cadringher explained how Group S would have worked.

'After many meetings with the manufacturers we arrived at the conclusion that we've got to stick to around 300bhp. Ten cars will be the minimum, but it's not impossible that the manufacturers will build 20 or 30, all strictly identical, which must be homologated and cannot change during that year.

'There will be no evolution during that year, but it will be no problem for the following year – just produce ten cars at the beginning of each year. That puts each manufacturer on the same footing at the beginning of the year.'

However, before Group S had begun the world of rally had been turned upside down by a series of tragic accidents. The first came on the Portuguese Rally in 1986, where Joaquim Santos lost control of his Ford RS200 over a rise and careered into a group of spectators, killing three and injuring 31. More tragedy was to follow on the Tour de Corse, when Lancia's star driver Henri Toivonen and co-driver Sergio Cresta were killed in a fiery crash. When Marc Surer's co-driver Michael Wyder was killed in another high-speed accident in an RS200 on the ADAC Rallye Hessen, FISA decided it had to act and outlawed Group B for 1987, with Group A imposed in its place.

The decision was broadly welcomed, but

many within the sport were still pushing for Group S rules to be adopted. A letter from Lancia's works drivers to FISA read:

'The drivers totally support FISA's efforts to control both spectator and driver safety, but we feel that the current proposals will not achieve the desired results and would request that consideration be given to the following points:

- The drivers are very concerned about the use of turbochargers from both the safety point of view and that of control of power in rallying.
- The drivers are very concerned about the use of plastic and inflammable materials in current rally cars.
- The drivers agree with FISA's objective of a maximum power in rally cars of 300bhp but wish to point out that current Group B cars have developed many safety features by way of suspension, steering, brakes etc, which will not be available in Group A cars.
- We recommend that the use of slick tyres be completely banned in rallies.

'Given all the previous points, we believe that a total change to Group A for World Championship rallying is not a solution to all the problems that currently exist. Many manufacturers without suitable Group A cars will be forced out of the sport and, as a result, we would respectfully request that FISA gives consideration to a Group S formula with the following major characteristics:

- Normally aspirated engines, maximum power 300bhp.
- No plastics or inflammable materials.
- Limitation on aerodynamic devices.
- A crash test for all rally cars.
- Minimum production qualification that will allow as many manufacturers to contest World Championship rallies as possible.

'With the introduction of the measures listed above, the drivers believe that safety in rallies will be greatly improved without destroying the stability of our sport.'

Their calls fell on deaf ears, and the World Rally Championship for 1987 ran to Group A rules as FISA wished.

The rules initially required the building of 5,000 models of the cars, although this was reduced to 2,500 in 1993. The cars had to use the same bodyshell and general dimensions as the road cars upon which they were based, with the engine also taken from the same unit used by the road cars. In general, this meant:

- Four-wheel-drive transmissions.
- 2-litre turbocharged engines using a 38mm turbo restrictor.
- Front-mounted engines (longitudinal or transversal).
- Minimum weight of 1,230kg.

The rules did permit modifications to the base car in the following areas:

- Full suspension geometry and layout. The original mounting points must be preserved within a 20mm radius.
- Engine internals including camshafts, crankshaft, valves. Other engine components can be machined. The engine block must be preserved.
- Engine peripherals (radiators, intercoolers etc).
- Engine management.
- Braking system.
- Gearbox, gear ratios, number of gears and gear selection type.
- Differentials.
- Final-drive ratio.
- Electric equipment.

The death of Group B led to Audi and Peugeot withdrawing from the WRC, leaving the 1987 championship to be fought out between Lancia and Toyota, although Audi did return with the Audi 200 Quattro. Mazda also joined the fray with its 323 turbo, while a number of Group A touring cars were converted into rally spec and found their way on to the stages.

Group A initially kept speeds and costs under control and ensured the survival of the sport at a time when that was uncertain. The cars might not have been as spectacular as the Group B beasts that preceded them, but, as marques like Ford, Mitsubishi and Subaru inevitably got involved, pretty soon they were every bit as fast.

Chapter Two

The Subaru Impreza in action

From the 1993 1000 Lakes through to the 2008 RAC Rally, all of the highs and lows, mud, sweat and tears of the Subaru Impreza World Rally Championship programme is described in the following pages. In total, there were three drivers' championships, 47 wins and over 1,000 special stage wins.

OPPOSITE **Pierro Liatti at full flight on the 1995 Rally Argentina.** *(Prodrive)*

1993 – the Impreza's Group A debut

The work that had commenced on the Impreza programme in January 1993 was demonstrated to the world when a pair of the blue and gold machines joined the start of the 1000 Lakes Rally on 27 August that summer.

Although the 1000 Lakes was no longer the sole preserve of the Flying Finns as had been the case before Carlos Sainz and Didier Auriol triumphed there, a bit of local knowledge still went a long way in one of the fastest and most challenging events on the calendar, and Prodrive certainly had plenty of that in the shape of Markku Alen and Ari Vatanen, who between them had amassed a total of nine 1000 Lakes wins.

Testing had been promising and there was a great sense of anticipation of a good result heading into the event. However, the rally had barely begun when the two-car squad was reduced to a single-car entry when, on the opening stage – Valkola – Alen made a

mistake, ploughed into the trees and caused terminal damage to the steering. The team was understandably furious, and according to *The Rallying Imprezas* John Spiller suggested over the radio that Alen should leave his overalls in the forest too, to the disbelief of the mechanics listening.

Alen couldn't believe what had happened: 'Maybe I'd gone too soft with the compound of my tyres,' he recalls. 'It was early in the morning, and at that time after every stage we would have service. And I had very special tyres for the early morning. There was a lot of moving from the rear and I lost control and we had a big crash. I was very upset with what happened, but it was my mistake.' It would be the last time Alen competed for the team, although he was called upon to work on the testing programme on a couple of occasions thereafter.

Juha Kankkunen had won the opening stage for Toyota, while Vatanen completed the Impreza's first competitive stage in third, six seconds down on his countryman and behind his Toyota teammate Auriol. It was the same 1-2-3 on Stage 2, with the Impreza losing just

BELOW The Imprezas undergo preparation ahead of their full WRC debut at the 1993 1000 Lakes Rally.
(Prodrive)

three seconds to Kankkunen's pace-setting Celica over 15km of the Lankamaa stage. It took just three stages for Vatanen to register the Impreza's first stage win, clawing back one second on Auriol and two on Kankkunen over the 16.85km of Kalliokoski.

Auriol took his first stage win of the event on SS4, ahead of Kankkunen and Vatanen, while Vatanen scored his second stage win on SS5 as the same trio continued to dominate the event. Auriol headed SS6, while Vatanen claimed his third stage win on SS7 and backed it up with another win on SS8 to move into second place overall. Kankkunen was back to the fore in SS9, but Auriol reclaimed second place overall with victory on SS10.

Kankkunen went on a roll with back-to-back stage wins on SS11 and SS12, while victory for Vatanen on SS13 drew him level on time with Auriol, ten seconds back from the leader on the overall classification. He won again on SS14, and even though the Frenchman went fastest on the final stage of the day it wasn't enough to prevent the two Finns from leading the way as the opening day drew to a close.

Classification after Leg 1:
1 Kankkunen.
2 Vatanen +7s.
3 Auriol +10s.

To put their dominance into perspective, Tommi Makinen in the Lancia Delta HF Integrale in fourth place was over two minutes behind!

Leg 2 began with Vatanen winning the 23.61km Leustu stage, reducing Kankkunen's lead to just five seconds. Kankkunen reasserted control over the 30.54km of super-fast 'yumps' through Ouninpohja, but for the first time in the rally there was a different name in the top three as Makinen beat Auriol into third. The Frenchman responded by winning the next stage, where the top three were covered by a single second!

Vatanen kept up the pressure on Kankkunen by winning SS19, while Auriol showed he was still a factor by triumphing on SS20. Vatanen was on top in Salvo, as Kankkunen was back in equal third with the Mitsubishi Lancer Evo 1 of Kenneth Eriksson. However, Vatanen then had his worst classification of the rally so far

BELOW Vatanen showed the Impreza's potential with a stunning 1000 Lakes performance. *(LAT)*

when he found himself back in fifth over the short, 2.60km of Tampere, finishing behind the Lancers of Eriksson and Armin Schwarz and falling 12 seconds behind Kankkunen on the general classification.

That gap stretched out to 16 seconds as the Toyota teammates set identical times on SS23, but this was the cue for an epic charge by the 1981 World Champion. He took four seconds out of Kankkunen over SS24, and a further four over SS25. He felt like he was driving as well as he'd ever done, but still he trailed his compatriot by eight seconds. But that was erased in one fell swoop as he beat Kankkunen by 11 seconds over the 21km of Vaheri. On its first event the Impreza was leading the way and giving Toyota's all-star line-up a real headache.

As darkness was falling Juha Kankkunen retook the lead with victory on SS27, and Vatanen's inspired charge effectively ended on the final stage of the day as he dropped 15 seconds to Kankkunen on Surkee.

The problem was that by fitting the bonnet-mounted auxiliary lamp pods the team had unwittingly played havoc with the car's aerodynamics, and meant that rather than sucking air in, the air scoop was blowing it out, which had a most unexpected and unfortunate consequence.

'I started the stage and I thought "How unlucky can I be? It's raining not for Juha but for me",' recalls Vatanen. 'But in fact it wasn't raining, it was water coming from the intercooler, because when they put the lamps on it created such turbulence that the scoop that was supposed to take air in actually pulled the air out. And the injector that was just behind the scoop, instead of injecting water into the intercooler it was coming out and on to the windscreen! So A, I lost power, and B, the windscreen got misty and I had to use the wipers. After that I was like a balloon that's deflated – there was no rally left for me any more.'

The way things had been going up to that point convinced Vatanen that he could have put up a real fight for the win: 'I was making no mistakes, but still I couldn't catch Juha – I couldn't make more than four seconds of difference,' he says. 'And then we had this

service halt, and instead of speaking to people as I would normally I went with my brother-in-law and had a hot shower and I was out of sight. Then on the following stage, Vaheri, I beat him by 11 seconds, and I think that must be one of the very best stages of my life. I at least had a psychological edge over Juha because of those 11 seconds over 20-odd kilometres. And that minute at the end, it doesn't reflect the real result.'

Auriol's challenge also ended on that final stage of Day 2 as he damaged the car's suspension and oil cooler with a heavy landing over a jump. This left Kankkunen with a relatively straightforward task of wrapping up the victory over Leg 3. There was one more stage win for Vatanen – his 15th of the event – ensuring he brought the Impreza home for a fine second place, an unrepresentative 47 seconds behind the winner.

The Impreza wouldn't be seen in action again until the RAC Rally in November, but the warning shots for its rivals were loud and clear – here was a car that was going to be a very serious contender.

ABOVE Vatanen in action on the 1993 RAC Rally. *(Prodrive)*

BELOW McRae had his first WRC outing in the Impreza on the 1993 RAC Rally. *(Prodrive)*

1994 – building the foundations

McRae gave the Legacy a fitting send-off by guiding it to Subaru's first World Rally Championship victory on the 1993 New Zealand Rally, and with it allowed Prodrive to usher in the era of the Impreza. For the 1994 season McRae was joined in the team by double World Champion Carlos Sainz, who after a disappointing season with Lancia was a free agent and the logical choice to partner the spectacular and explosive Scot.

The experienced Spaniard had an almost instant and positive effect on the team, not only bringing additional funding through his Repsol backing but also by accelerating the development process through his thorough and meticulous approach to testing.

As David Richards was quoted in *The Rallying Imprezas* as saying: 'Carlos, I would say, was one of the key people that galvanised the team, because there was no denying his work ethic and professionalism. And he came along at a time when things were starting to come together very well.

Some drivers sit back and say "My job is to drive the car, their job is to run the team and run the test programme." Carlos wanted to be involved in everything. He would want to be involved in all the testing, he would be the last one there on a test session, he would be the one who pushed Pirelli to get the tyres right for us, he would be the one that drove everybody just that little bit harder, just to get the best out of things.'

The mechanics were inspired by his determination and attitude and it pushed them on to raise their game too, so perhaps it should have been no surprise that it was the Spaniard who claimed the Impreza's first WRC win.

Sainz began his Subaru career with a third on the Monte, fourth in Portugal and second place on the Tour de Corse, a rally he was leading comfortably until a front anti-roll bar snapped on the final leg, gifting the win to Toyota's Didier Auriol.

Next up was the Acropolis in Greece. With Pirelli's tyres working to perfection the Imprezas were in a class of their own. Initially it was McRae leading the way, but following a mid-race spot-check by the officials they

ABOVE The crowds gather to watch the Prodrive team get to work in Portugal in 1994. *(Prodrive)*

LEFT Sainz in action on his home event – the 1994 Rally Catalunya. *(Prodrive)*

LEFT McRae led Sainz on the 1994 Acropolis before misfortune struck. *(Prodrive)*

failed to refasten the bonnet pins. The Scot had barely got out of second gear when the bonnet flew up and smashed the windscreen. Lacking sufficient time to replace the screen without incurring time penalties, the rally was delayed as the officials dealt with the furious McRae, who argued that as they had caused the problem he should be given the time needed to get it changed without fear of any penalties. Eventually this request was granted, but the Scot's chance of victory ended later that day when he hit a rock and damaged a wheel bearing.

LEFT Sainz delivered the Impreza's maiden win on the 1994 Acropolis. *(Prodrive)*

BELOW LEFT McRae was spectacular in Argentina, but crashed out of the rally. *(Prodrive)*

BELOW Sainz and co-driver Luis Moya celebrate second place in Argentina. *(Prodrive)*

This left Sainz free to stroll home for the Impreza's first win. McRae's second place, however, did not stand, as the officials accused him of blocking the road and preventing other cars from starting. He denied the charge, but his cries fell on deaf ears and he was excluded from the event.

Following a wheel-tearing accident in Argentina, compounded by McRae dragging the three-wheeler along for a further ten miles, causing even more damage, the pressure was starting to mount on the Scot to start delivering results. He responded with a magnificent performance in New Zealand. Prodrive's new active front diff was ready, and though the part wasn't actually fitted to the car just yet the optimal settings that had been refined in testing were put on the car, and McRae used them

to fine effect to beat François Delecour by 27 seconds and seal his first win in the Impreza.

The decision had been taken before New Zealand not to send McRae to the 1000 Lakes, leaving Sainz to bring home the sole Impreza in third place. McRae was back again for Australia, and once again he was in unstoppable form, although the rally didn't form part of the World Championship and was instead a round of the Asia Pacific series.

Sainz was still in contention for the championship, but when his title rival Didier Auriol beat him into second place on the penultimate round of the season in San Remo it meant he would need all the help he could get if he was to turn the deficit around on the RAC event. Prodrive rejected the notion of employing team orders, but these became unnecessary

BELOW Richard Burns was called up to the WRC squad for the 1994 Rally New Zealand. *(Prodrive)*

ABOVE Third place on the 1994 1000 Lakes kept Sainz in the title hunt. (Prodrive)

RIGHT McRae dominated the 1994 Rally Australia, although it was not a WRC round. (Prodrive)

ABOVE Burns pushes on in the 1994 Rally Australia. *(Prodrive)*

LEFT Burns played a key role in Subaru winning the 1994 Asia-Pacific title. Here, he kicks up the dust in Thailand *(Prodrive)*

RIGHT Sainz was a solid second on the 1994 Rallye San Remo. *(Prodrive)*

BELOW McRae took his second WRC win of 1994 on the RAC Rally. *(Prodrive)*

when Sainz's rally ended in a ditch and McRae was free to score an emotional home win in front of his adoring fans which put him very firmly on the front foot for the 1995 season.

1995 – World Championship year

The FIA introduced a raft of technical and sporting changes for the 1995 season. On the sporting side the points system was altered, requiring each manufacturer to enter three cars per rally, with the scores of the best two making up the final tally. This meant McRae and Sainz would be joined by three new drivers: Richard Burns, the 1993 British Rally Champion for Prodrive, who'd campaigned the Group A Impreza in the Asia-Pacific Championship during 1994; Italian Piero Liatti, an asphalt specialist and the 1991 European Champion; and Subaru veteran 'Possum' Bourne, who'd won the 1994 Asia-Pacific title in an Impreza.

On the technical side the main change was the shock decision to reduce the turbo restrictor size from 38mm to 34mm, rather than 36mm as had been expected. The other technical change was the outlawing of full slick tyres, with the new regulations stipulating that 17% of the tyre had to be treaded. Both these changes meant the cars were slower and had less grip, something that left the drivers unimpressed but achieved the FIA's goals of curtailing speeds. Finally, there were changes made to the servicing rules, preventing cars from being worked on after every stage and only allowing the support teams to operate within the designated service parks.

Monte Carlo

Defending champion Auriol led the 198 starters away for the first stage of the 1995 season-opening Monte Carlo Rally, but on the damp, ice-free stage it was the Imprezas that instantly held sway, with McRae immediately establishing a five-second lead over Sainz, while Ford's François Delecour slotted into third and 'best of the rest'. However, on the snow-coated second stage McRae made a mistake and dropped two minutes as, with the help of some spectators, he and co-driver Derek Ringer dug the Impreza out of a ditch.

ABOVE McRaes senior and junior celebrate Colin's 1994 RAC win. *(LAT)*

'There was a wee ditch and I dropped in,' he told *Motoring News* at the time. 'I reckoned it would come out in reverse, but they were pushing for about a minute and it wouldn't come out, and then I found I'd got it in first, not reverse.'

Sainz went quickest on SS2 and again on SS3, which, while largely dry, had patches of snow, ice and slush. Almost all the crews had opted to run studded tyres and Pirelli's rubber choices were proving to be the equal of anything the conditions could throw at them.

As the snow and ice gave way to rain as the rally headed north, Delecour fought back in splendid fashion, taking a huge chunk out of Sainz's 47-second lead with victory in SS4 after making the inspired decision to de-stud his tyres by hand, while most of his rivals chose to leave the studs in place.

McRae took his second stage win of the event on SS5, but Delecour was back on top on SS6 and homing in on Sainz out front. Delecour survived a scare when his car refused to fire up in the next service park. Despite the full Ford crew being on hand they were unable to touch the car and had to look on helplessly as Delecour's co-driver Catherine François gave the 1,300kg Escort a push-start.

Victory on SS7 meant that Sainz ended the day with a healthy 44-second lead, but the rally was coming down to pot-luck on tyre choices and he was worried that one wrong call could instantly undo all of his advantage. After his

earlier travails McRae was back in ninth, but at least the car had escaped undamaged.

Ice and snow abounded as the rally headed into some of the highest stages of the event at the start of Leg 2. Sainz made the correct tyre call and his narrow ice tyres were the perfect match for SS7, but they didn't help at all on SS8, where the snow covering was much thinner. Wearing the studs down caused him to spin and allowed the charging Delecour to claw back 39 seconds in one go, and when he went fastest again on SS9 the Frenchman led the rally for the first time.

With no tyre change permitted before the next stage Sainz was stuck with his sub-optimal tyre choice. Pirelli's clever stud bonding now proved to be its undoing as there was no way of removing the studs, while the Michelin drivers were busy unpicking theirs ahead of the largely snow- and ice-free 20km asphalt stages that lay ahead.

Ford wisely used the time in between the stages to fit larger front brake discs to Delecour's car, and pulled another 20 seconds on Sainz over SS10. But as dusk descended and the temperatures dropped Sainz fought back, winning the penultimate stage of the day and clawing back a further 21 seconds on Delecour by a last-minute gamble to run RT55 slicks on the final stage of the day, which was won by Delecour's Ford teammate Bruno Thiry. Delecour himself had made the wrong call by running with studs and ended the day 26 seconds in arrears, but the rally had barely reached its halfway point and there was no way Sainz could be confident that his advantage would stick.

McRae had been driving swiftly and worked his way up the order to sixth place. However, on the day's final stage he was caught out by a patch of ice on a fifth-gear corner and slid off the road, coming to a rest about 30ft away down a slope. The car was not badly damaged, although the radiator had been split, but there was no way of getting it back on to the stage and McRae's rally was over.

'OK, so it's just a bad corner,' he told

Motoring News. 'We didn't know that. We'd slowed down even more, because it was the last stage of the day, but how much slower can you go?'

Ironically, McRae's new teammate, Piero Liatti – making his Monte Carlo debut – had gone off at exactly the same corner and had radioed back to the team with a warning. Despite significant damage to the right-hand side of the car from where he'd hit a post the car was at least still running, although the Italian was now down in 17th place.

Sainz started Leg 3 by setting the best time on SS13, creeping a further second ahead, but Delecour closed the gap down by 12 seconds on SS14 as once again tyre choice became the defining factor.

Juha Kankkunen claimed his first stage win of the rally as Delecour pulled back yet more time over SS15. He was eight seconds quicker than Sainz again on SS16 as Thiry took his second stage win of the event.

With only 90 miles of stages left to run Sainz's lead was down to just 12 seconds, but next up was the famous Col de Turini, the highest stage of the rally, almost half of which was covered in thick ice. Despite this Sainz gambled on running the RT55 slick and it proved to be an inspired choice. Delecour had chosen a harder compound and dropped 17 seconds to the Spaniard but showed that he wasn't going to give up when he out paced Sainz by three seconds to win SS17, and when the master switch died and caused Sainz's car to unexpectedly cut out mid-stage in SS18 it showed just how vulnerable his lead was. His quick-thinking co-driver Luis Moya jammed it back into place and spent the rest of the stage reading his notes with one hand.

The master switch was bypassed for SS19, but there was no need to panic. Delecour's car had suffered a broken shock absorber on SS18, and the Frenchman dropped over a minute to his rival. His fight for a second Monte Carlo Rally was over and Sainz was able to ease off for the remaining three stages (all of which were won by Kankkunen's Toyota) and claim his 15th WRC win.

Liatti kept his nose clean after his earlier accident and rose up the order to eighth, meaning that Subaru trailed Ford by just a single point in the manufacturers' standings.

Rally Sweden

Local ace Mats Jonsson was drafted into the Subaru line-up for round two of the 1995 championship, Rally Sweden, where, using his local knowledge, he backed up Sainz to come home second on SS2 as once again the Impreza established an early advantage. But it wasn't the Ford Escorts who were taking the fight to Subaru this time but the Mitsubishi Lancers of Kenneth Eriksson and Tommi Makinen, and as their red and white cars started to stretch their legs out in front Sainz started slipping down the order after a flying start, so that by the end of Leg 1 it was McRae leading the Subaru charge.

ABOVE McRae's 1995 Monte Carlo Rally ended in a ditch. *(Prodrive)*

BELOW McRae led early on in Rally Sweden, but all three Imprezas retired. *(Prodrive)*

Sainz's cause wasn't helped by a detour off the road at a quick left-hander, which required around 30 seconds and the help of a group of spectators to get him back on the road. However, much worse was to follow as he waited to enter *parc fermé* at the end of the day. Without warning, the engine suddenly spat out its oil.

Much to many people's surprise, Sainz started Leg 2 having changed the oil filter himself following a quick lesson from the Prodrive crew. Remarkably his car made it through the opening stage, despite leaving a trail of the black stuff in its wake, but when it dumped the remains of Repsol's finest when it was fired up for SS10 there was no option but to retire the car from the event.

McRae, meanwhile, was trying to keep the Lancers in sight from third, although a quick spin on SS9 didn't help his cause. He'd chosen to run Pirelli's experimental SB35 snow tyres, but these were designed for deep snow so weren't working in the conditions encountered on the event – a situation exacerbated by the new tyre rule preventing him from changing them at the end of the morning's running.

Jonsson's rally ended while he was ahead on the opening stage of the final leg, when like Sainz's it dumped its oil in one dramatic spurt. McRae's car wasn't looking too great either, and, sure enough, it came to an oily halt as he desperately tried to limp to a service area.

'We think it's a fairly simple problem,' Lapworth told *Motoring News* at the time, 'but the consequences are pretty drastic. Little bits of debris jammed the oil pressure relief valves closed and blew the oil cooler seals; it blew the oil cooler seal or the seal around the block. I'm not unduly concerned.'

Rally Portugal

The dusty, rocky roads of Portugal were in stark contrast to the snow of Sweden, but the real test would be whether the Subaru's engine would be up to the job in one of the most exciting rallies of all time.

The Toyota of Juna Kankkunen flew out of the traps, setting the pace on four of the opening five stages. The sole interloper was Sainz, who was fastest on SS4, but the feeling was that the Subarus were distinctly down on power. 'There is no power,' Sainz told *Motoring News*. 'It was the same in the test and they said it would be better for the rally. No response, no torque, no power.' McRae was equally unhappy, although a spin on the opening stage had left him back in fourth place.

Richard Burns was making his seasonal WRC debut in the third Impreza, but by SS4 the Brit was already in trouble with a slipping clutch. He managed to limp it on for a further two stages until the snapped clutch spring could be changed, losing around a minute and a half in the process.

The mid-Leg break gave everyone a chance to take stock, and Sainz regrouped and responded by winning SS8 and SS9, clawing back six seconds of Kankkunen's advantage. Heavy rain in the build-up to the rally meant many of the stages were very muddy and Sainz made the decision to switch to a stiffer damper to handle the conditions. His charge was also aided by Kankkunen hitting a rock and damaging the steering arms of the Celica, despite which he still managed to set the fastest time on SS10. But when Sainz charged through the 16.62 miles of Sao Lourenco 14 seconds

BELOW Burns brought his Impreza home in seventh on Rally Portugal. *(Prodrive)*

faster than the Finn the Subaru star was in the overall lead for the first time in the rally.

Auriol had set the fastest time on SS7 to briefly demote Sainz from second place, but he was 40 seconds back by the end of the Leg though still ahead of McRae, who was in a disappointing fourth place and battling with a thirsty intercooler spray that was requiring top-ups with water after each stage. The power-sapping issue was traced to a loose relay on the pump. Burns, meanwhile, was running eighth and just trying to keep his nose clean and stay out of trouble.

Yet again the Toyotas shot out of the blocks at the start of Leg 2, with Auriol and Kankkunen fastest in four of the first five stages. Sainz was mystified by his inability to match their pace and switched back to the softer dampers in an effort to get back into the fight. After setting the pace on the opening two stages of the Leg, Auriol's challenge was ended when he rolled on SS14. It cost him a minute and he slipped behind McRae and into fourth.

The Scot had had a spin on the final corner of SS12, but following the repair of a faulty air temperature sensor he went on to record his first stage win of the event, setting the pace in SS15 and out pacing Sainz for three stages in a row. Burns persevered with his safety-first approach and held on to eighth. By the end

of the Leg, Sainz was trailing Kankkunen by 22 seconds, while McRae was over a minute behind in third with Auriol breathing right down his neck.

There was damp on the roads as the drivers set off for the final Leg and this played into Pirelli's hands. Its K66s were perfect for the conditions, and over just two stages Sainz carved 18 seconds off Kankkunen's lead. As the rain intensified Kankkunen opted for some hand-cut Michelins and threw caution to the wind to win SS26 and SS28 (27 was cancelled), extending his lead to 12 seconds.

Almost all of this advantage was wiped out when Sainz produced a stunning run on SS30 to outpace Kankkunen by 11 seconds. Having taken a second off the Finn on the previous stage – which was won by Armin Schwarz – the two drivers were now level on time, with only three stages and 23 miles of the rally left to run.

Both drivers were giving it everything, and arrived wide-eyed at the end of each stage with tales of how near and how often they'd come close to having an accident. But it was Sainz whose nerve held the best, opening up a two-second lead with victory on SS31. He stretched that by a further seven seconds on SS32, leaving Kankkunen with an almost insurmountable gap to chase down over the final 6.4 miles of Figueiro dos Vinhos.

ABOVE McRae's first points of 1995 came with third place in Portugal. *(Prodrive)*

But less than a mile into the stage Sainz cut a corner and a log went through the front spoiler and broke a brake pipe. With no front brakes, he had to complete the stage using only the rear brakes and transmission to slow the car. Amazingly he actually won the stage! 'It was very, very close,' he told *Motoring News*. 'It was a fantastic race. I thought I had lost it – I can't believe it!'

McRae finished a distant third, while Burns moved up to seventh when the privately entered year-old Celica of Marcus Gronholm crashed on SS26.

Tour de Corse

Things didn't get off to a great start for the Subaru team on the twisty roads of Corsica. Sainz felt his engine was down on power, and by the end of the second stage he was already half a minute behind the early leader, Ford's Bruno Thiry. To make matters worse he lost pressure in the central diff, which would have

to wait until the mid-Leg break before it could be repaired.

McRae, meanwhile, was less than impressed with the new asphalt tyres, which the regulations decreed had to have at least 17% tread. Liatti was back in the third car, and following all of Sainz's issues was running ahead of the former World Champion.

Things didn't improve in the afternoon. A power steering leak caused McRae to spin on SS6, while Sainz and Liatti were busy tweaking the suspension set-up in search of a better balance. A valve change fixed Sainz's diff and the Spaniard upped the pace and ended the Leg in fifth as the leading Subaru. Liatti was sixth and McRae seventh, with just three seconds covering them.

Pirelli's decision to bring the RC35 and RC55 tyres was leaving the Subaru drivers between the devil and the deep blue sea: the 35s were too hard and the 55s too soft to make it through a stage without significant drop-off. This meant that rather than fight Thiry and Auriol for the overall win, all three Impreza drivers were locked in a battle with the Mitsubishi of Andrea Aghini for third.

Liatti took his first stage win as he dominated SS12, something he attributed to the firmer suspension option he selected, and he ended the Leg in fifth place, just a second behind Sainz in fourth. McRae was just a few seconds further back in seventh.

The Subaru drivers were again in tyre trouble as Leg 3 got under way, and within three stages both Liatti and Sainz had been passed by Aghini.

There was late heartbreak for Thiry as a broken wheel bearing denied him victory in an event he had dominated. Auriol inherited the win – a record-equalling sixth on the event – while Sainz was promoted to fifth and McRae sixth after the team instructed Liatti to take a penalty at the final time control so that the Scot scored an addition two points.

New Zealand

A shoulder injury sustained while mountain-biking meant that Sainz was forced to miss the New Zealand Rally. It meant that Burns received an unexpected call-up to join local favourite 'Possum' Bourne in the team's line-up, but it would be Subaru's other Brit who the headline writers would be talking about after the event.

Having won the previous two WRC rounds held there, McRae went into New Zealand full of confidence, and he played himself in slowly. It wasn't until the penultimate stage of the opening Leg that he recorded his first stage win of the event, and he was back in fifth place in the overall classification, 11 seconds behind rally leader Tommi Makinen. Meanwhile transmission issues had blighted Burns and restricted him to eighth place, while Bourne was struggling to get to grips with the reduced power of the 34mm turbo-restricted cars.

ABOVE In Corsica, Liatti gave up a place to help McRae boost his score. *(Prodrive)*

Heavy overnight rain had soaked the stages, but this didn't stop Makinen taking off like a rocket and winning the first three stages of Leg 2. But perhaps he was pushing too hard, since on SS10 – Mahoe – his rally was over, his Lancer stuck at the bottom of a steep bank. McRae, in contrast, leapt from fifth to first over the stage's 20 miles. 'That was the stage that was going to tell the difference,' McRae reckoned in *Motoring News*. 'If Tommi was quicker there we could forget it.'

With the soft Pirelli K67s fitted to his car for the first time on the rally, McRae was quickest by 15 seconds and moved into a clear lead. In addition Subaru was running the active centre diff on the car for the first time and it was proving to give much improved turn-in and traction.

With a rough wheel-speed sensor having been identified as the cause of his handling issues, Burns was showing his credentials too. He was second only to McRae over the 17.23 miles of Tuha, which moved him into sixth place overall, only for a puncture on the next stage to cost him ten seconds, which allowed Delecour to reclaim the spot.

Three stage wins in a row had hinted that perhaps Auriol and Toyota could challenge McRae, and a further stage win on the final run of the day meant he ended the Leg just 12 seconds behind the Scot.

McRae clipped a bank on the opening stage of the final Leg, but the minor damage this caused would not distract from his *coup de grâce*. SS19 was held over 27.82 miles of Motu. More overnight rain had made the stage very slippery, but this only played into McRae's hands, and over the next 38m 9s he effectively won the rally. He was 35 seconds clear of the rest, which meant his overall lead was now 47 seconds. It had been a masterclass in rally racing, and a hat-trick of Rally New Zealand wins was now his to lose.

'I drive the Motu almost as though it's a tarmac stage,' he revealed to *Motoring News*, 'brake really early, turn in off the brakes, which you don't normally do on gravel, so you keep

it straight and you can get the power early, so you can get the traction … It's really just long and twisty. It's not a particularly enjoyable stage – it's just the time at the end of it!'

Motu would be the undoing of Burns' charge. Midway through the stage he braked for a ford, but the force of the water tore the radiator off its mountings, which took with it the alternator and power steering belt. The car kept going until the battery finally packed in nine miles from the finish.

McRae was fastest again on the next two stages, and his rivals were spared another beating as the reverse run of the Motu stage was cancelled. He ended Leg 2 with a lead of 1m 3s over Auriol, who in turn was well clear of Kankkunen in third. Bourne was running in the top ten in the third Impreza, but was treating the rally as a test run after accepting that it was impossible to catch any of the cars running ahead of him.

Given the gaps between the top three there wasn't much at stake over the final Leg. McRae was fastest on SS27 to consolidate his position. Having played around with the front differential settings, Bourne suddenly found the Impreza much more to his liking and he was second to Auriol on the final two stages of the rally, taking an eventual eighth place.

But the star of the show was McRae, who'd not only scored his first win of the season but had also kick-started his title challenge. In Sainz's absence the championship lead had passed to Auriol, who was on 51 points, one ahead of Sainz and Kankkunen, who were level on 50. McRae was a further ten behind in fourth place.

Rally Australia

The six-week gap between New Zealand and the next round in Australia gave Sainz plenty of time to return to full fitness and rekindle his search for a third world title.

With Kankkunen performing his usual heroics down under it was left to McRae to take the fight to the Toyota driver on the opening Leg of the Rally Australia. However, despite being happy with the performance of the car and Pirelli's K48 tyres McRae was lucky to still be in the event at all after a hard impact with a bank on SS6, which left his Impreza with a

remodelled boot. The incident was blamed on a faulty intercom between him and co-driver Derek Ringer, and the batteries were duly changed for the next stage.

Sainz struggled to get to grips with the loose surface and complained of the gearbox tightening over the course of the long stages, so that by the end of the Leg he was back in fifth place as the first tranche of stages drew to a close. Things were considerably worse for Bourne, however, who slid off the road on SS3, took a wheel off on a tree and that was his rally over.

BELOW With Sainz absent, New Zealand victory was crucial for McRae. *(LAT)*

Sainz was in trouble on SS8 – the 28-mile Wellington Dam run, where a branch lying across the road punctured the Impreza's radiator. Sainz and Moya made whatever running repairs they could manage, but the engine had run dry and there was still over half the stage to run to the emergency service park.

Sainz had lost 12 minutes. A new radiator was added and he set off on SS9. However, the car was smoking ominously, hinting at a blown engine. Sure enough the car cried enough before it made it to the next stage and Subaru was reduced to a single car before the first Leg had even run its course. But McRae was still up

and running, and he beat Kankkunen over the next two stages to close within nine seconds of the leader. However, the Finn responded by reeling off three fastest stage times in a row to establish a first Leg lead of 17 seconds.

The McRae/Kankkunen party was gatecrashed at the start of Leg 2 by the Mitsubishi Lancer of Kenneth Eriksson, who won SS14 and SS15 to force his way into the battle at the front. McRae fought back with stage wins on SS16 and SS18, to eke out a small two-second lead over the Swede. Kankkunen, however, was struggling to keep up, and despite winning the final stage of the day the Leg 1 leader had by then slipped to fourth, over a minute behind Eriksson.

Overnight rain had made the stages slippery for Leg 3 and McRae was soon caught out, losing valuable seconds when he locked up and stalled on SS23. But he fought back with a victory on the next stage. However, a spin and damaged rear wheel thanks to contact with a rock had cost him a further nine seconds, and the Scot's hopes of recording back-to-back wins were looking slim.

Eriksson was equal to whatever McRae could throw at him over the final sequence of stages to claim his fourth and most impressive WRC win to date. Second place moved McRae into second position in the championship, ahead of Sainz for the first time. Kankkunen

now led the way, but with just 14 points covering the top five there was no telling which way the pendulum might swing next.

Rally Catalunya

Having failed to score in the previous two rallies, the pressure was on Sainz to hit back in his home event. However, the 1995 Rally Catalunya would prove to be one of the most controversial in the history of the WRC…

The rally started with Toyota's Juha Kankkunen setting the pace and Sainz leading the charge behind him, despite a quick spin on SS8 that cost him ten seconds. McRae also had a spin on SS8 but was still running a competitive fourth, close to his target of third place in the event. The two Subarus were split by the second Celica of Armin Schwarz who was going great guns on the Spanish asphalt, taking four stage wins out of nine on the opening Leg.

There had been some rain during this Leg, with McRae in particular getting caught out on SS4, but it was much damper on Leg 2, and this was destined to have an impact. Kankkunen was setting the pace again, and an incorrect gamble on the hardest compound Pirellis played a part in Sainz dropping 17 seconds across SS12 and SS13.

Kankkunen appeared to be out of sight now, and Sainz also had a fight on his hands to keep hold of second from the charging McRae.

A broken driveshaft had meanwhile brought Schwarz's impressive run to an end. In the third Impreza Liatti was enjoying a strong run, despite a faulty hydraulic pump on the centre differential meaning that it was only possible to run with four-wheel drive by running it as a locked unit, which did nothing to improve the car's handling. Still, he was running well inside the points, ensuring that Subaru was leading the way in the manufacturers' fight.

However, the rally was turned on its head on the final stage of the day when Kankkunen misheard 'bad left' as 'fast left' in his pace notes and skidded off the road. The Celica was left upside down and wedged against a tree so that he and co-driver Nicky Grist had to kick out the windscreen to escape the battered car. Nevertheless, with the help of a group of nearby spectators they actually managed to right the car and get it going again. But 52 minutes had been lost, along with any hope of victory.

Subaru now found itself running 1-2, a healthy distance clear of Didier Auriol in third. Despite McRae having closed to within five seconds of Sainz, David Richards made the call to impose team orders, effectively preventing the Scot from challenging for the win. 'It's not fair to have team orders,' Sainz told *Motoring News*. 'We should just leave it, even though it would be good for me.'

ABOVE Sainz won Rally Catalunya following a controversial finish. *(LAT)*

McRae was understandably incensed: 'It's crazy, you've got two drivers fighting for the World Championship – and Carlos isn't that slow on the RAC,' he ranted at *Motoring News*. 'I'm sure there will be a discussion tonight. It'll probably go in one ear and out the other.' Subaru tried to calm the situation, issuing a statement late that night that read: 'It's not team orders: it's an agreement between the drivers and the team.'

The events of the day had promoted Liatti into fourth, but the final Leg would prove to be even more explosive…

If McRae intended to honour the team's instructions it wasn't apparent at the start of the day, as he halved Sainz's overall lead with victory on SS18 and reduced it to a single second after topping SS19. He took the overall lead during SS20, which was won by Auriol, who was showing that he shouldn't be written off too readily either. McRae stretched his lead further as Auriol won again on SS21, and with just two stages of the rally to run things were getting strained in the Subaru ranks.

Auriol's charge ended with power-steering failure, which Liatti – running with a fresh gearbox in his car – took full advantage of to make it a Subaru 1-2-3. But which one would be the winner?

Heading into the final stage, McRae led Sainz by eight seconds and made it plain to his teammate that he had no intention of moving over and letting him win. Prodrive sent team manager John Spiller along with Nigel Riddle and John Kennard to the flying finish, with a board instructing McRae to slow. But the Scot barely lifted, let alone slowed, and on the timings he had won the rally by nine seconds. However, following some heated negotiations and the involvement of Colin's dad Jimmy, McRae was finally persuaded to incur a minute's road penalty by booking into the time control late.

'If we have a problem on the RAC, we'll lose the championship,' an irate McRae told *Motoring News*. 'I don't see why there should be team orders when there are two drivers fighting for a World Championship. We were going at the pace we were going at, which was a very comfortable pace and it's very difficult to change – you might make a mistake. I would rather not win the World Championship than win through team orders.'

Sainz restated his unease with team orders in the post-race press conference, but was equally unhappy with McRae's behaviour: 'The only tactic is win or crash. I don't know if I could beat Colin. He has driven a fantastic rally

BELOW McRae won Rally Catalunya on the road but was instructed to pick up a time penalty. *(LAT)*

and I congratulate him. It is not easy to accept team orders and at first, I did not agree. If it has been decided from yesterday like it has been, it is not very nice what happened today. What is not very nice is the behaviour of Colin ... it is affecting my relationship with him.'

With Liatti in third Subaru should have been celebrating its first 1-2-3, but instead the team was trying to quell an outbreak of civil war. Still, it could have been worse – they could have been in Toyota's position.

Following a routine check, irregularities were found around the turbo restrictor on Auriol's car. FIA technical delegate Jakko Markkula released a short statement that left no doubt that this was a serious offence indeed:

- The restrictor is not sealed, which means it is possible to move it without touching the sealings.
- All the air may not pass through the restrictor.
- When the restrictor is moved to its longest position, the rule of the maximum distance of 50mm is not respected.

Basically, Toyota had flouted the 34mm turbo restrictor and was giving its cars an unfair power advantage. Auriol was excluded from the rally, but far worse was to follow, as upon further investigation the FIA felt the rules breach was sufficiently heinous to warrant exclusion from the 1995 championship and a 12-month ban from the WRC.

RAC Rally

Sainz and McRae headed into the final round of the season tied on 70 points apiece. And with Toyota having been expelled from the championship, the title would be a straight fight between the teammates in a winner-takes-all battle to the finish.

The Spaniard's quest for a third world title got off to an ignominious start as he ruptured the Impreza's radiator through Chatsworth ford. It was a well-known weak point of the Impreza and with so much at stake it was a critical error.

It was the Mitsubishis of Tommi Makinen and Kenneth Eriksson that were leading the way. Four straight stage wins at the end of the Leg meant it was Makinen who was out in front by

11 seconds, while Eriksson – who led briefly after winning SS3 – was second. McRae had had a brief spell at the front after winning SS2 at Chatsworth, but more importantly he was 14 seconds up on Sainz. In the third Impreza, Richard Burns survived a whack with some straw bales that bent his steering column, but was lucky to still be in the rally.

On the opening stage of Leg 2, McRae shot into the lead of the rally, thundering through the 17 miles of Hamsterely half a minute faster than any of his rivals. Makinen had hit a log and lost a minute as he dragged his car through the stage with collapsed suspension and a broken driveshaft. But the damage proved too great for the team to repair, and one of the Subaru's key rivals was out. However, McRae's lead would be short-lived, as two miles into the next stage he clattered a rock and picked up a puncture. 'We drove for maybe ten miles, but then the tyre went soft,' he explained to *Motoring News*. 'The EMI was OK, but then the tyre came off the rim.'

With Eriksson hitting the same rock and experiencing the same fate, Sainz found himself in the lead, although things were far from cosy inside L555REP, as the car was starting to overheat, a legacy of his radiator issue from Leg

BELOW Sainz pushed hard on the RAC Rally, but it would all be in vain. *(LAT)*

1. Sainz was now 1m 14s ahead of McRae, but there was no way the Scot was going to give up without a fight.

He took 11 seconds out of Sainz over the next stage and a further four on the one after that. On Kershope he only managed to reduce the Spaniard's advantage by two seconds, but then again he had hit a rock mid-stage and forced the right-front wheel into the arch. There was damage to the strut and the lugs as well as a deflated tyre. But the suspension was hammered back into shape and McRae was back on his way. Eriksson was fastest on SS12 before McRae took back-to-back wins through the Grizedale forest stages, taking a further 18 seconds back on Sainz. 'We are on the limit. We can't go any quicker without taking risks,' McRae admitted to *Motoring News*. Burns had now worked his way up to fourth in a great tussle with the Ford Escort of Bruno Thiry.

From 1m 14s behind, McRae had managed to cut his gap to Sainz to just 39s, and with the damaged front-right corner completely repaired overnight he went into Leg 3 full of confidence, winning the opening two stages of the day to take a further 18 seconds out of Sainz's lead. The Spaniard recovered a little with his stage

win on SS17 – only his third of the event – in which he regained two seconds.

Hydraulic fluid was leaking from the seal on McRae's centre diff from the opening stage. This was causing the pressure to drop and hurting the balance of the Impreza's handling. Nevertheless, he stormed to another stage win, a remarkable 12 seconds faster than Sainz, on SS18, while he removed another second from the lead on SS19.

McRae's fifth win in six stages reduced the lead to only five seconds, and with Prodrive having remapped the ECU for the central diff the car was now handling much better too. This was the cue for another masterclass through the ruts of Sweet Lamb, and suddenly McRae was leading the rally by 17 seconds.

With Eriksson putting a huge dent in his Lancer after contact with a gate Burns was now up to third, and for the second rally in a row Subaru was on the brink of a clean sweep of the podium.

McRae's gearbox was changed overnight and he headed into the final Leg determined to put the rally to bed in the opening stages. He eked his lead out by just two seconds on SS22, but when he went 11 seconds faster than Sainz in Dyfi, *El Matador*'s resolve was broken and it was now just a case of McRae bringing the car home in one piece. Sainz did take two more stage wins as McRae backed off, but it was the Scot's day and he and Derek Ringer celebrated becoming Britain's first ever WRC champions. Third home was Richard Burns, completing a perfect event for the team with his first WRC podium.

'Mentally, this was a greater success than Catalunya was,' he told *Motoring News*. 'It was a real battle, but more for myself. Although I wasn't actually fighting with anyone, I just had to catch up and not make any mistakes. It was an equally good performance because of that.

'Once you've done it once, you want to do it again. It can be harder the second time. One of the things I'll try and do now is to be very quick on all the rallies. Most of the drivers now specialise in a few events. Carlos would perhaps be the one driver who you would say was very good overall. The only weakness I have is tarmac events at the moment.'

LEFT Not quite smiles all round as the Subaru boys celebrate McRae's title win.

(Prodrive)

helping McRae to defend his championship, and, equally importantly, Subaru to retain its manufacturers' crown. For the first time ever four works Imprezas were entered for the season-opening Swedish rally, with Toyota refugee and 1994 World Champion Didier Auriol joining McRae, Eriksson and Liatti in an expanded line-up.

Mitsubishi's Tommi Makinen led from start to finish to claim a comfortable win over Sainz. McRae set eight fastest stage times to kick his title defence off with a third place, while Eriksson was fifth on his Subaru debut. Auriol scored the final point in tenth place, but would never drive for the team again.

Subaru had brought Alen in from the cold to undertake an extensive Safari Rally preparation, which included the introduction of beefed-up suspension, in particular the Bilstein struts and longer gearing.

1996 – the final season for the Group A Impreza

Given the events over the final two rallies of 1995, it should have been no surprise that Carlos Sainz was looking for a new seat for 1996, reasoning that Subaru was now very firmly McRae's team. Toyota's 12-month ban meant he took a two-year detour to Ford before rejoining the Japanese manufacturer for 1998. While he would win eight more times, never again would he mount a significant title challenge.

After his stunning performance in Australia, Kenneth Eriksson was now very much considered to be a top-line WRC driver, and Prodrive pulled off something of a coup to wrest him away from Mitsubishi to join Piero Liatti in

Eriksson was a strong second, but he was a long way down on Makinen, who dominated the event at the first time of asking. McRae finished fourth despite almost losing a wheel at one stage, while Liatti was fifth as Subaru matched Mitsubishi point for point in their duel for manufacturers' honours.

Sainz claimed his first win for Ford to prevent Makinen making it a hat-trick in Indonesia. Both McRae and Eriksson crashed out – McRae while leading comfortably – so Subaru's hopes rested with Liatti and he rose to the challenge to take second place.

LEFT McRae was a solid fourth on the Safari. *(Prodrive)*

LEFT New signing Kenneth Eriksson was second on the Safari. *(Prodrive)*

BELOW Eriksson was brought in after Sainz left for Ford. *(Prodrive)*

McRae finally recorded his first win as defending champion as he beat Makinen in a head-to-head fight on the Acropolis. The rally was a real tyre-eater, and Pirelli's rubber handled the conditions better than Michelin's. McRae had a small scare when he started to notice a vibration from the propshaft, but the team managed to get it changed in under ten minutes and he was able to continue his winning run unhindered. Liatti was fourth and Eriksson fifth as Subaru extended its lead in the manufacturers' standings.

McRae found himself in hot water with the FIA after the next round in Argentina. After he'd damaged a rear crossmember in an accident with a rock, the lengthy time it took to change the part meant he was running late as he headed for time control. The area was packed with spectators, and as he pushed on in an effort to minimise his time loss he ran over three of them. Fortunately none of them was injured, but the FIA took a dim view of the goings on and later fined him $75,000 after his actions were reviewed in a tribunal in Paris. Makinen, meanwhile, took his third win of the season ahead of Sainz and Eriksson, while Liatti finished seventh.

There was yet another crash-induced retirement on the 1000 Lakes, and with Makinen strolling to yet another win McRae's title defence appeared to be over before the halfway point of the season. Eriksson was fifth as the team entered just two cars for the first time in the season.

LEFT Eriksson was on the podium again: third in Argentina. *(Prodrive)*

LEFT A big crash on the 1000 Lakes ended McRae's title hopes. *(Prodrive)*

BELOW Eriksson examines his car on his way to second on Rally Australia. *(Prodrive)*

Another Makinen win next time out in Australia meant the Mitsubishi man sealed the title with two rounds still to go. Eriksson was second, McRae a distant fourth, Liatti seventh.

McRae ended the season with back-to-back wins in San Remo and Catalunya to at least secure second place in the standings and help ensure that Mitsubishi was beaten in the manufacturers' fight. Eriksson was a solid fifth in Italy, while Liatti pushed McRae all the way in the season finale, eventually finishing just seven seconds down on the outgoing champion.

After 11 WRC wins, one drivers' championship and two manufacturers' titles, the Group A Impreza had come to the end of its competitive life – at least at WRC level. The

ABOVE Eriksson ended the 1996 season with seventh place in Catalunya. *(Prodrive)*

car had proven to be a great all-rounder with no real weaknesses, except a propensity for radiator damage in fords.

But this was far from the end of the Impreza story. In fact, its successor, the Subaru Impreza WRC97, had already been launched a few days earlier…

The WRC era

The World Rally Car regulations were introduced by the FIA in 1997 as a way of encouraging more manufacturers to enter the sport. While the rules still required the cars to be based on production models that had been built in quantities of 2,500 and over, the range of modifications that were permitted, from engines to four-wheel-drive and sequential transmissions, meant that there was no need for the creation of 'homologation specials'. Instead, manufacturers that didn't have a suitable model among its existing range could 'up-spec' one of its cars into a WRC competitor. As a result, cars such as the Peugeot 206, Skoda Fabia and Citröen Xsara were able to compete in the WRC despite there being no four-wheel-drive, 2.0-litre petrol turbocharged car available to buy.

The wraps came off the first Prodrive-built

RIGHT McRae gave the Group A Impreza a fitting sign off with victory on Rally Catalunya. *(Prodrive)*

LEFT Liatti took his
maiden win on the
WRC Impreza's debut
in Monte Carlo. (LAT)

Impreza WRC car ahead of the 1996 Rally
Catalunya in a glitzy event held in Lloret. The
blue and gold paintwork remained, but this was
otherwise a very different-looking car – for a
start it had only two doors instead of four! WRC
rules allowed for much greater aerodynamic
freedom and Subaru had employed renowned
car designer Peter Stevens to give the car a
bolder, meaner, more aggressive look.

With the regulations only limiting crankshafts
and con rods, Prodrive had a free hand in
developing the engine, but instead it opted to
run a revised version of the Group A power
unit, with modified camshafts, cylinder ports
and combustion chambers. It resolved one
of the previous car's shortcomings by moving
the turbo, which allowed for a much improved
exhaust system. Moving the turbo also created
room for a huge air intake and the efficient
channelling of the enormous amount of air it
was able to suck in. Most of the development
work centred around maximising this airflow,
which, in tandem with a larger intercooler,
meant that despite the air restrictor being kept
at a mandated 34mm the power and power
delivery was hugely improved.

With the turbo now tilted through 20°
new exhaust manifolds were needed, which
finally allowed Prodrive to create even lengths
of manifold and even out the firing pulses,
although this meant the loss of the distinctive
boxer burble that had been such a fan favourite
on the Group A car.

The suspension layout remained the same
as the Group A car, with MacPherson struts
all around, but extended from 1,690mm to
the full limit of the regulations, 1,770mm. The
transmission and roll cage carried over, but
Prodrive took full advantage of the flexibility
of the regulations regarding the suspension
positioning, whereas the Group A version
had been compromised by the original strut
locations of the road car.

For the inaugural WRC-rule season Prodrive
retained the same line-up as in 1996 of McRae,
Eriksson and Liatti. And it was the Italian who
gave the Impreza a winning debut, claiming the
first victory of the new era – and his only win in
the WRC – on the Rally Monte Carlo. Eriksson
backed this up with his own first win for Subaru

BELOW Fabrizia
Pons, Liatti's co-driver
as they powered to
victory in Monte Carlo.
(Prodrive)

next time out in Sweden, while McRae made it a hat-trick of wins for the new machine by claiming his first Safari Rally win. McRae won again in Corsica, but both Imprezas retired with engine failure in Portugal – something that was proving to be a weakness in the WRC97.

McRae suffered an engine blowout while leading in New Zealand, although Eriksson picked up the pieces. The issue was eventually traced to the lightweight design of the camshaft drive. However, by the time the issue was addressed the title had been lost to Tommi Makinen and Mitsubishi, which had chosen to update its Group A car rather than build a bespoke WRC version. But three wins in the final three rallies ensured that for the third year in a row Subaru won the manufacturers' title.

The WRC98 featured a host of changes to the previous year's car with most of them made to the engine and exhaust system. These included a new crankshaft, flywheel and con rod, revised engine mapping with the adoption of anti-lag, a bigger turbo and revised exhaust manifolds. On top of this there were active dampers and, finally, fully active front, centre and, for Rally New Zealand, rear differentials.

McRae continued to lead the driver line-up although he was being tempted with a big-money move to Ford. Liatti was the mainstay of the second seat, although Eriksson drove one last rally for the team in Sweden, after which he was

ABOVE Eriksson claimed his first win for Subaru in Sweden. *(LAT)*

RIGHT McRae made it a hat-trick of wins for the Impreza in 1997 on the Safari. *(LAT)*

let go and headed to Hyundai. Local hand Jarmo Kytolehto partnered McRae in the 1000 Lakes, while a familiar face in the form of Ari Vatanen was part of a three-car entry at Rally GB that also included Colin's younger brother Alister.

McRae started the season with third place in the Monte Carlo Rally. He retired from the next two events, but victory on Rally Portugal brought him back into the title hunt. A broken diff forced

LEFT McRae ended 1997 with another RAC Rally win, but missed out on the title. *(Prodrive)*

BELOW LEFT McRae's first win of 1998 came in Portugal. *(LAT)*

BELOW Victory in the 1998 Rally Corsica thrust McRae into the title reckoning. *(LAT)*

him out of Rally Catalunya, but a win on the Tour de Corse meant he was still in contention.

He was going wheel-to-wheel with Tommi Makinen in Argentina when he hit a rock in the middle of the road and damaged the suspension. He performed a near miraculous roadside repair, and despite going on to win

the next stage with his bodged-up car he had checked into the time control two seconds late, and the subsequent time penalties dropped him to fifth.

Victory in the Acropolis Rally took McRae into the lead of the World Championship. But he was a distant fifth in Australia after Subaru's

first turbo failure in five years denied him victory. He crashed out of the 1000 Lakes and was a disappointing third – behind Liatti – in San Remo. Meanwhile Makinen was racking up the wins, and heading into the Rally GB finale the momentum was with the Finn.

Typically McRae put on a charge in front of his home fans and was leading the rally when his engine fell sick and a marvellous eight-year stint with Prodrive and Subaru came to a smoky end.

Prodrive blended youth with experience when it recruited Richard Burns and four-time World Champion Juha Kankkunen to lead its ranks in 1999, with Belgian Bruno Thiry playing a supporting role. Kankkunen began his Subaru career with a fine second place on the Monte in the WRC98, but the new WRC99 was introduced in time for Rally Sweden. The biggest change was the introduction of a new gearbox, spelling the end of the H-pattern unit that had begun its life in the Legacy. In its place came a high-tech hydraulic system operated by steering-wheel-mounted paddles. In addition there was a raft of electronic updates, including a fly-by-wire throttle and new engine software that allowed for full-blown traction and launch control.

Burns was the best-placed of the three Impreza drivers with fifth on Rally Sweden, but none of the cars made it to the finish on the Safari. Burns was fourth in Portugal but by mid-

ABOVE Engine problems ended brought McRae's time at Subaru to an inauspicious end. *(LAT)*

BELOW Bruno Thiry drifts his way to 10th place on the 1999 Rally Sweden. *(Prodrive)*

RIGHT **Four-time champ Juha Kankkunen took his first Subaru win in Argentina.** *(LAT)*

season the team was still searching for its first win with the new car.

It arrived in style, and controversy, in Argentina. Burns was leading comfortably and backed off to save the car, but Kankkunen opted to push on, ignoring the team's calls to ease off. Thus it was the 39-year-old who scored the WRC99's first win. A fired-up Burns responded with a determined win on the Acropolis.

Burns wrapped up the season with two wins and two seconds in the final five rallies, while Kankkunen would score the 23rd and final win of his career by leading home the Brit in Finland. Makinen's early-season form meant he was the champion yet again, but the wind was very much in Subaru's and Burns' sails heading into 2000.

Wins on the Safari, Rally Portugal and Argentina in the opening six rounds put Burns in control of the championship early on. The second of those wins had been achieved with the new car, the P2000, the first Subaru to be designed by Christian Loriaux, who set about improving the car's handling by repositioning the engine and gearbox and saving weight wherever possible. Even the driver was seated lower down in the car as every effort was made to optimise the balance and weight distribution.

LEFT **Burns claimed his first win for Subaru on the 1999 Acropolis.** *(Prodrive)*

LEFT Burns was irked by Kankkunen in Argentina, but responded magnificently. *(Prodrive)*

ABOVE LEFT Kankkunen led home Burns for a 1–2 in Finland. *(LAT)*

ABOVE Burns flew to victory in Australia. *(LAT)*

LEFT Suspension damage ended Kankkunen's run in Australia. *(Prodrive)*

RIGHT Subaru's line-up for the 2000 WRC campaign. *(Prodrive)*

BELOW Kankkunen kicked off 2000 with third place on the Monte. *(Prodrive)*

RIGHT **Burns was victorious on the 2000 Safari Rally.** *(Prodrive)*

However, when Burns needed to push on mid-season the WRC2000, to give it its official name, let him down. There were damper issues on the Acropolis, shattered flywheels in New Zealand and driver error in Finland, where he rolled out. Kankkunen, meanwhile, was struggling to get to grips with the car at all and scored just three top-three finishes all season and not a single win.

Makinen's disqualification from victory in Australia ended his reign as champion and all-but assured Marcus Gronholm his first world title. Burns scored a commanding win in GB to

LEFT **Jean-Joseph Simon was spectacular on his way to seventh in Corsica.** *(Prodrive)*

LEFT **Gearbox issues ended Petter Solberg's Rally Corsica.** *(Prodrive)*

RIGHT There was a dramatic new look for Subaru in 2001. *(Prodrive)*

BELOW Engine issues hobbled Burns on the 2001 Monte Carlo. *(Prodrive)*

once again end the season on a high. And this time it would not be a false dawn.

Subaru introduced a new Impreza for 2001, the bug-eyed 44S. It was the first four-door Impreza since the Group A car of 1996, but underneath it owed a lot to the P2000. However, gains had been made in terms of stiffness and especially aero performance.

Young Norwegian driver Petter Solberg had joined Subaru for the final two rounds of 2000, and despite crashing out of both events he was promoted to a full-time drive alongside Burns. Another young driver – Estonian Markko Martin – would fulfil third driver duties alongside Japanese veteran Toshihiro Arai.

Initially the WRC2001 was plagued by reliability issues. Burns suffered with a down-on-power engine in Monte Carlo, hit a snow bank in Sweden and had hydraulic issues in Portugal. His season was finally kick-started by a pair of second places in the space of a month in Argentina and Cyprus, but he went off while heading for a top-three result on the Acropolis, and when broken suspension forced him out of the Safari on the opening Leg his championship hopes seemed over.

LEFT Markko Martin crashed out of Rally Portugal. *(Prodrive)*

Loriaux left for Ford and Prodrive reshuffled its engineering department. Second place for Burns in Finland was followed by a great win under pressure in New Zealand to set up one of the most open title races in history. When McRae rolled

out of Rally GB, third place was enough for Burns to win the championship.

Burns joined Peugeot for 2002, but only following an out-of-court settlement after Prodrive pursued a breach of contract suit. It hired four-time champion Makinen to replace

ABOVE LEFT Martin had a disappointing season, scoring just three points. *(Prodrive)*

ABOVE Burns's sole win of 2001 came in New Zealand. *(Prodrive)*

LEFT Burns' New Zealand win underscored his 2001 title charge. *(Prodrive)*

ABOVE Makinen began his Subaru career with victory on the 2002 Monte. *(LAT)*

ABOVE RIGHT Solberg was fifth on the 2002 Rally Corsica. *(LAT)*

RIGHT Solberg took third place on Rally Australia in 2002. *(Prodrive)*

BELOW Victory on the 2002 Network Q Rally was a sign of things to come for Solberg. *(Prodrive)*

him, while Solberg was given another season to prove himself after a disappointing 2001.

Makinen won on his debut in Monte Carlo but was forced out by engine failure in Sweden.

The WRC2002 was introduced for the Tour de Corse. It featured a new turbo and other engine tweaks, but was visually very similar to its predecessor save for a new front splitter.

Six retirements in the next seven rallies killed any hopes Makinen might have harboured of a fifth title, but the Impreza was struggling to match the pure pace of the Peugeot 206. Makinen was fighting for the win when he crashed heavily in Argentina. This promoted Solberg into second and it would be the Norwegian who led the Subaru attack in the second half of the season, when three podiums in the final four rallies – including a stunning maiden win on Rally GB – announced Solberg as a player on the world stage.

Subaru had a facelifted, prettier car for 2003, but the changes for the WRC2003 were more

RIGHT High spirits ahead of the 2003 Monte, but both cars would crash out. *(Prodrive)*

than just cosmetic, with significantly improved aero. The team even developed an active suspension version of the car, although that was quickly banned before it had a chance to prove itself. The team line-up for 2003 was the same as the season before, but Solberg had now firmly established himself as the lead driver.

BELOW Subaru's new-look car was rolled out ahead of the 2003 season. *(Prodrive)*

ABOVE LEFT Subaru and Prodrive celebrated 10 years together in 2003. *(Sutton Motorsport Images)*

ABOVE Cheers! The 10-year partnership party took place at Rally Australia. *(Prodrive)*

LEFT Solberg capped the anniversary with a fitting win. *(Prodrive)*

BELOW LEFT A year after his break-through win Solberg captured the title. *(Prodrive)*

BELOW Makinen was third in Australia on his final rally for Subaru. *(Prodrive)*

RIGHT Solberg was fourth on the 2004 Rally Mexico. *(Prodrive)*

BELOW Solberg and new-for-2004 team-mate Mikko Hirvonen. *(Prodrive)*

BOTTOM A flamboyant Hirvonen was seventh in Japan. *(Prodrive)*

Wins in Cyprus, Australia and France meant he went into the Rally GB finale needing to beat Citröen's Sebastien Loeb in a straight fight to win the title. His cause was aided by early retirements for Gronholm and Sainz, and with Pirelli supplying the ideal tyre Solberg duly repeated his win from the previous year to beat Loeb to the title by a single point. Makinen coming home third gave everyone involved at Prodrive and Subaru plenty of reason to celebrate.

Burns had initially been rehired for 2004, but sadly the brain tumour that would ultimately take his life prevented him from ever driving the car. In his place Prodrive recruited a promising young Finn called Mikko Hirvonen.

Solberg opted for a safety-first start to his title defence, banking the points in Monte Carlo and Sweden. The WRC2004 came in for round three in Mexico and while very similar from the outside the biggest change came in its switch to TAG electronics.

Wins in New Zealand and Greece meant that Solberg kept pace with Loeb in the first half of the season. However, a broken radiator in Argentina, accident damage in Finland and a huge crash in Germany allowed the Frenchman to open up a significant points lead. A hat-trick of wins in Japan, GB and Sardinia nevertheless showed the car and driver had the pace, but with Loeb finishing second all three times it barely dented his points advantage and Solberg would have to be content with the runner-up spot in the standings.

Solberg gave WRC2004 a winning send-

off in Sweden and the new wide-track WRC2005 a debut win in Mexico to take the championship lead. Loeb then went on a six-rally winning streak that killed the championship. Solberg added another win on Rally GB, which was enough to ensure that he beat Gronholm to second place in the championship on countback.

Hirvonen was replaced by Chris Atkinson and the Australian repaid Subaru's faith with his maiden podium in Japan. Ex-Formula 1 driver Stephane Sarrazin was also given a handful of outings, scoring a best result of fourth in his home event in France.

There was another significant redesign

on the WRC2006, as well as a series of rule changes that outlawed active diffs and water injection. The changes seemed to hit Prodrive especially hard and WRC2006 suffered the indignity of being the first works Impreza that failed to win a rally. The same three drivers contested the rallies, but only Solberg cracked the top three, finishing second in Mexico, Argentina and Australia.

Things didn't improve with the WRC2007. It featured a host of changes under the bonnet, especially to the radiator and intercooler, but there were just two podium finishes, both scored by Solberg. The WRC2007 carried over for the first six rounds of 2008 as Prodrive readied the radical new WRC2008.

Atkinson got the season off to a strong start with second place in Monte Carlo and was third on the inaugural Rally Jordan. The new car hit the stages for the first time in the Acropolis. Since it was first introduced the Impreza had been a saloon car. However, with the trend in road car sales moving away from four-door to five-door cars the GE model was launched exclusively as a hatchback. Although a saloon would join the range later, it was a five-door Impreza that appeared at the Acropolis. The more compact bodyshell featured less overhang, which should have made for better handling, and on its debut Solberg delivered an encouraging second place. But that would be as close as it got to winning. Atkinson added

BELOW Solberg works his way to seventh on the 2006 Rally Acropolis. *(Prodrive)*

LEFT Solberg gave it his all on his way to fourth on the 2007 Rally Norway. *(Prodrive)*

CENTRE Despite Solberg's heroics, he could only muster sixth in Germany. *(Prodrive)*

BOTTOM Atkinson kicked off 2008 with third place on the Monte. *(Prodrive)*

another podium in Finland, but on 16 December 2008 came the shock announcement that Subaru would be leaving the WRC with immediate effect.

'Fuji Heavy Industries Ltd (FHI), the maker of Subaru automobiles, today announced the withdrawal from the FIA World Rally Championship (WRC) at the end of the 2008 season,' read the official statement.

President Mori commented that reaching this decision had been an extremely difficult task, not least with regard to the countless Subaru fans that for many years had cheered the legendary Subaru blue-liveried Impreza World Rally Car: 'We would like to express our sincere appreciation for our fans' strong and loyal support worldwide. They will remain an invaluable treasure for us.'

After 19 years, three drivers' titles, a hat-trick of manufacturers' titles, 47 rally victories and 1,215 stage wins, the dream was finally over.

'We went into a difficult period in 2008,' says Richards, 'as did all the Japanese manufacturers, and instead of holding true to their heritage and what we'd managed to create they decided to become the same as everybody else, and there are too many brands out there producing competent cars at a similar price and you need to have very distinct brand values if you want to retain an audience and retain brand loyalty. It was quite extraordinary. And to me the great sadness is that it [the change in brand perception]) hasn't been capitalised on. They've lost the impetus.'

Subaru might have lost the differentiator that rallying success gave the brand, but the memory of the Impreza, especially the Group A version, remains to this day.

LEFT An Impreza hatchback! Aktinson retired on the GE's debut. *(LAT)*

BELOW The end of the road: Solberg on the Impreza's last WRC outing –the 2008 Rally GB. *(Prodrive)*

Chapter Three

The anatomy of the Group A Subaru Impreza

From the Pirelli tyres, the development of the active diffs, the water cooled brake calipers, not to mention the ultimately doomed attempt to produce a pneumatic H-pattern semi-automatic gearbox, and of course the various developments that were required to get the best from the unique boxer engine, this chapter looks under the skin of the Group A Impreza.

OPPOSITE The famous Subaru boxer engine and all its ancillaries. *(Adam Warner)*

Chassis

A central component to every racing car is the chassis. And while the demands of the rally stages might reward aggression rather than finesse, it's still imperative that the handling of the car is stable and predictable if the driver is going to have the confidence to throw it into a blind corner. Equally as important is that it's safe and strong. Even the best rally drivers become unstuck at some time, and a car that can survive the odd bent panel – or worse – is a must.

As is the case for a great deal of all the Impreza's underpinnings, its design was very much informed by the lessons that had been learned on the Legacy project, which Prodrive oversaw from 1990 onwards, and the man in charge of making the Legacy, and the Impreza, a rally winner was David Lapworth.

Lapworth has been a part of Prodrive for almost as long as the company has existed. Initially he *was* the engineering department, but by the time work had commenced on the Subaru project he was heading up a small band of talented and passionate engineers. Now he's the company's technical director. However, he recalls the process that went into taking the knowledge gleaned from the Legacy and using

BELOW Getting the Impreza ready for its 1993 debut at the Prodrive factory.
(Prodirive)

it to inform the basis of the chassis construction for the Impreza.

'The learning curve was very steep at that time,' he says. 'Most of the people in the team had a fair amount of rally experience, but it was our biggest project by far to do the Legacy from scratch. Period. So whilst we brought a fair amount of experience to it, it was all-new.

'We had been running the Legacy for the best part of three years by the time we started on the Impreza, and I thought we'd sorted it out pretty well. I think we'd got a good grip on it, but it needed a step up, so we were really keen

to get on with doing the Impreza, because we liked what we saw.

'When we were shown the new car it addressed a lot of the things that were out of our control. The Legacy was a bit on the big side – you only have to look at the size of the WRC VW Polos and so on to realise that with a clean sheet of paper you probably wouldn't go quite as big as a Legacy.'

Compared to the Legacy, the Impreza was 170mm shorter and 15mm narrower. Despite this, and how it appeared to the naked eye, the Impreza's wheelbase was only 60mm less. With a lighter, nimbler car, Prodrive had a great

BELOW The final checks take place as the cars are readied for the 1993 1000 Lakes. *(Prodrive)*

opportunity to take the best bits of the Legacy and improve on its weaknesses.

'The Legacy was very easy to drive, very stable and so on, but we felt that we needed to do something new and the Impreza came along at just the right time,' Lapworth adds. 'The bit that stalled things a little was a bit of hesitation from Japan because they didn't want it to look like we were moving from the Legacy out of necessity. They didn't want to make the Legacy look like a loser and the Impreza a winner, because they were still selling the Legacy. But we eventually got going and I felt we did a pretty good job of addressing the things that needed to be addressed and carried over the things that we'd learnt. We didn't do a completely new car but we did address everything we wanted to considering the resources and the timescale we had.'

Lapworth and his small team, which comprised Bob Farley, Ian Moreton, Mick Metcalfe and Graham Moore, started work on the Impreza in January 1993. Most of the suspension and the steering rack were carried over from the Legacy. These had been developed for the previous two years, so were proven items and it meant that more attention could be paid to the areas that needed it the most.

'We had a smaller car, so we took the opportunity to try to lower the inertia, lower the centre of gravity,' Lapworth explains. 'A lot of it was repackaging the Legacy into a smaller car. Sitting here now, I'd say I guess 50–60% of the car was genuinely new, and 50% was carried over and refreshed. We probably reviewed virtually every drawing. Some things would have been passed straight across, but others would have needed to be a little bit lighter, some a little bit longer, but we didn't go right back to basics on very much.

'The biggest thing was the reduction in size and the reduction in the moment of inertia – the car was a lot more responsive, which you could tell from the first drive. I drove the car up at MIRA on the first shakedown of the test car. I took it out for a few laps of what we used to call the Dunlop circuit – the one next to the control tower – did a couple of laps around there and by the time it was warmed up, even going at 80% of competitive speed I remember coming back with a smile on my face saying, "This is definitely the way to go, we've made a step here." It felt like this was what we were looking for.'

As a much shorter car, but with a similar wheelbase, the Impreza had an instant benefit over the Legacy, and that was a much lower moment of inertia. This is a key factor in the handling of a car as it defines the speed and agility with which the car turns, as Lapworth explains: 'If you go back to the basics of vehicle dynamics, people get very confused

RIGHT The importance of ensuring the chassis is strong is demonstrated by this Chris Atkinson crash in 2008. *(Prodrive)*

with the benefits of short wheelbase and the benefits of low inertia. A long wheelbase is good and low inertia is good, and they usually go with each other.

'The car is made up of thousands of pieces, but if you simplify it and think of it as a dumbbell that's made of two masses, one at the front and one at the back, the two added together equal the 1,200kg of car, but the length of that dumbbell makes a big difference to that moment of inertia.

'The car is always going to weigh 1,200kg but if the mass is concentrated in the centre of the car it rotates very easily. But if it's all out at the extremities, it becomes lazy. All the basic layout of cars – not just the wheelbase – has a big influence on that.

'If your engine, like an Audi in those days, is hanging over the front, you're staring at a disadvantage with the moment of inertia. And with a four-wheel-drive car you have a rear diff and associated hardware right at the back. Obviously with the Legacy, which is long wheelbase, those masses are even further apart.

ABOVE Creating a car that is strong and agile is key to rallying success. *(Prodrive)*

LEFT The Group A Impreza was strong on most surfaces, but especially gravel. *(Prodrive)*

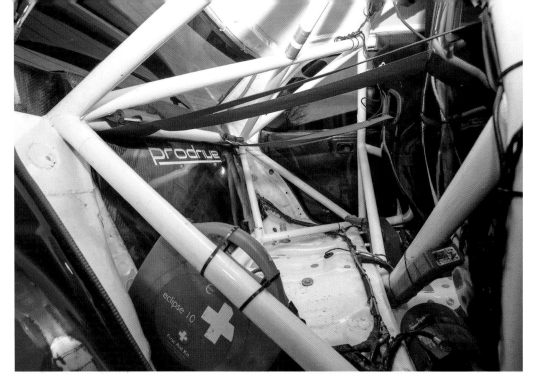

RIGHT A great
illustration of the
complexity of the
Impreza roll cage.
(Adam Warner)

'So by their nature, smaller cars tend to have lower inertia and the holy grail is a small car with a long wheelbase. So in the Impreza's DNA it was a more responsive car. The layout was similar with the engine and gearbox but the radiator wasn't as far ahead and the tail pipe wasn't as far behind, and that brings it all down. So the inertia reduced a lot more than the wheelbase did. The wheelbase wasn't much different, but there was probably a foot chopped off both ends.'

As well as having a fundamentally smaller car, Prodrive took advantage of its new car by reviewing the design and placement of the crossmembers. These help to define the strength and stiffness of the chassis. The team set out with some critical engineering targets for road cage stiffness, lateral stiffness of the bodyshell, torsional stiffness, camber stiffness and toe stiffness. Key to all of this was making the crossmembers stiffer and lighter. Again this helps to reduce the inertia and make it more responsive.

The proof that Prodrive had done a good job with the Impreza's chassis came straight out of the box when Ari Vatanen had his first competitive run it in ahead of the car's debut on the 1993 1000 Lakes.

'We took the car to Finland because that was going to be the launch event,' Lapworth recalls, 'and Ari did a morning in the Legacy to get in the groove and set a benchmark, and after lunch we swapped to the Impreza, and he did a couple of runs and came in with a big

smile on his face, saying "Yes! This is the way to go." I can't remember the time, but it was significantly faster. And the smile on his face – that counts for a lot!'

A Group A rally car fundamentally starts its life from the same place as a mass-production road car. So if a specialist constructor like Prodrive wanted to make any fundamental modifications they had to try to put pressure on the manufacturer to compromise what they might do in production. This gave rise to cars like the Ford Sierra Cosworth, which has a turbo that was really too big for everyday road use, as well as a rear wing that made no sense away from the white-hot world of competitive motorsport.

'It was always to Subaru's credit in some ways that they were not prepared to go as far down that homologation special journey as some other manufacturers might have been tempted,' says Lapworth. 'They had a degree of – you could call it integrity, but certainly inflexibility in terms of meeting their normal engineering standards with every car they produce. They weren't as prepared to go as far as, say, Toyota or Ford would have done to make a special car. But on the other hand, considering the number they built, it was a bloody good car to start with. And I think history says that. They weren't homologation specials – you could buy one and the car you bought was actually pretty good.'

The car upon which the 1993 WRC version of the Impreza was based was codenamed

GC8A. Launched in late 1992, and called the WRX in sales brochures, it featured an aluminium bonnet with aggressive-looking air scoop, a more sporty-looking grille, a deeper front spoiler with integrated fog lights and a new rear wing.

The WRX was 10mm shorter than the standard car and also had lower ground clearance. Thanks to a host of weight-saving measures, such as reduced soundproofing, manual windows and no ABS, the car weighed approximately 30kg less than the rest of the range too.

Because the car was smaller and lighter than the Legacy, Prodrive was able to have greater flexibility with where it positioned the ballast than had been the case before, while still ensuring the car met the 1,230kg minimum weight. This resulted in an improved weight distribution of 55:45 front/rear split.

In Brian Long's book *Subaru Impreza* the late Colin McRae is quoted as saying after his first test: 'Compared with the Legacy, the Impreza feels quite different. It feels quite nervous to start with – it's twitchy and changes direction a lot quicker. The Impreza is certainly harder to drive, and I'm really trying to change my driving style to suit it. Nowadays you have to be so tight. Driving on a special stage is like driving on a race track – as soon as you start to slide around, you're losing time. The Impreza may feel like it wants to be driven sideways, but if you drive it straight it's going to be quicker.'

Internally, Prodrive had a very simple but effective system for determining where and how much could and should be invested in the development of the car. 'We had a very good formula for where we could spend money on the car,' says Moreton. 'There was a silhouette of the car and then there was some simple things: if it was revolving weight, or unsprung weight you could spend £600 a kilo. So you could spend a lot of money to save a lot of weight on the flywheel.

'At the other extreme – say a headlamp – that's outside the wheelbase, and relatively high up, so perhaps you could spend £200 per kilo on that. Inside the wheelbase and low down, you couldn't really spend much at all because you'd be bolting lead next to it, but anything outside the wheelbase or revolving or unsprung there was a table of what you could do, so

ABOVE **The distinctive front end of the Group A Impreza.** *(Adam Warner)*

engineering knew what it could do and where to focus the effort.'

An interesting fact is that in all Imprezas the tax disc was mounted directly on the roll cage rather than the windscreen. This was in case the windscreen got damaged and removed in an accident. Because the cars have to be taxed and registered for the road stages, especially in the UK, this meant that cars would still be legal even if the screen was missing.

BELOW A lot of Group A Imprezas feature aftermarket carbon door skins. *(Adam Warner)*

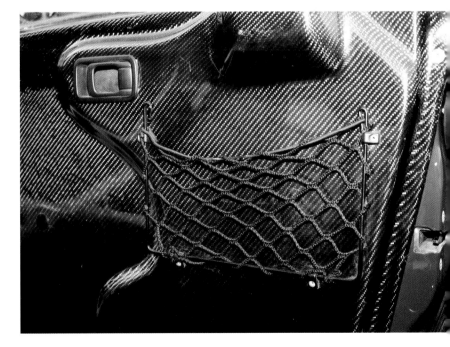

ABOVE **There wasn't a windtunnel programme, but the Impreza does have some aero features.**
(Adam Warner)

BELOW **By the end of the WRC era a full aero package had been developed.** *(Prodrive)*

Aerodynamics

Given that a rally car is almost as likely to be flying through the air as it is to be planted on the ground, there is clearly less of a need for the kind of trick aerodynamics that have become commonplace on just about every kind of track-racing car. But that's not to say that aero is not important, and while the extravagant wings and flicks that sprouted out of the Group B cars in the 1980s might not have been products of an extensive wind tunnel or CFD programme, they all shared a common aim – to make the car go faster!

Over the course of the Impreza programme – especially in the WRC era – more and more attention was paid to the aerodynamic properties of the car. However, this was still very much a black art. Cars on a rolling road in a wind tunnel are facing directly into the fan at a constant pitch, conditions that are almost non-existent on a rally stage. Also, in the tunnel the car is in perfect condition, something that tends to be as common and hen's teeth when rally cars return to the service park. So assessing the effectiveness of a new aerodynamic piece is complicated, while whatever its benefits are can only be felt if that piece is still on the car.

Making a rally car that's too aero-dependent would be a fool's errand.

'It's about learning how to make it durable, and it's a steep learning curve,' says Lapworth. 'I think all the manufacturers really started to wake up for the WRC era. Ourselves and Mitsubishi weren't bad and for sure we raised our game from the early Group A era to the WRC era. Certainly Peugeot showed that having a proper aero programme has a significant benefit. We really got our act together after seeing the performance of the Peugeot and going, "Right, now it's clear that the rally car needs clear aero targets like a race car. It doesn't carry the same weighting as a race car, but it's important enough to do it with the same rigour as you would with a race car."

'The challenge with a rally car is doing it with the ride heights and attitudes that rally cars have compared to racing cars. The big numbers in race cars tend to come from ground effects, and they are really difficult to exploit in a rally car. For sure there are aerodynamic effects of the underfloor that you have to take into account, so making the floor flat is a really good first step. Before that it's purely functional, it's protection. We played around with the shape of the front undershield to see if we could get any benefits, but without access to a wind tunnel and without CFD it was just "Try a few things and see if they make any difference".'

At the time of the Impreza Group A project, Prodrive was heavily involved with touring cars, firstly with BMW and then with Alfa Romeo. The Alfa in particular was part of the new breed of very aero-dependent touring cars, so it was only natural that some members of the rally project would be curious about the effect deploying some of that technology could have on the stages.

Prodrive didn't have its own wind tunnel at the time, so what little aero testing took place was done at MIRA. Eventually Prodrive started to recruit aero guys from Formula 1 and investing in CFD capabilities, but this was long after Group A had been consigned to the history books. Before that point it was a case of trying to make the car fast by other means.

'We had a bit of a sniff around wing mirrors – they are relatively small beer but you do need to do it,' says Lapworth. 'We were trying to understand cooling system layouts, which again isn't massive numbers but you might as well get them right as get them wrong. The big ones are the front bumper/splitter and the rear wing and wheel arches, that's where the big numbers come from, but because of the Group A rules it wasn't on the agenda anyway. There wasn't a development programme for it because you had what you had. You couldn't stick a splitter on it, you couldn't stick a big rear wing on it, so we never really pursued the journey of examining the way the undershield fits to the front of the car or the way we ducted the radiator. We only looked at first principles.'

Suspension

While Group A rules gave only very little flexibility in the positioning of the suspension mounting, they gave some scope for development of the type of suspension – dampers, uprights and arms – that was used.

The Impreza itself offered a good base, with the WRX coming with fully independent suspension, which contained MacPherson struts at the front and coil springs at the rear. There were also anti-roll bars front and rear, and the shock absorbers contained a linear control valve too. But all of this was of little interest to Prodrive, who opted to carry over the fundamentals of the Legacy's suspension, which had been developed over three years and was a proven concept.

'Once we'd got up and running with the Legacy, one of our first priorities was reducing friction and gradually reducing suspension travel,' Lapworth recalls. 'It has an A-arm wishbone in a single piece. Later on if you look at the Mini they tended to use a track control arm and a compression strut. But we chose to run a lower A-arm on the Impreza and it worked very well. Then it's a conventional MacPherson strut, with the strut in line with the upright.

'The Group A regulations kind of dictate the amount of suspension travel you can get anyway as well as the fashion not being ridiculously long travel in those days, so you're probably in the low 200s.'

The amount of suspension travel was also limited by the rules dictating the height of the top mount. This creates a natural distance between the driveshaft and the turret top that defines the amount of suspension travel that is possible, regardless of how much would be the case in an ideal scenario. 'The first target was to increase the suspension travel but mainly to reduce the friction,' says Lapworth.

This friction – or 'stiction', as it's sometimes called – is an inherent problem with the MacPherson strut. This reduction in movement hinders the wheel travel and reduces traction. Prodrive spent a lot of time developing this part of the suspension, concentrating on making fine detail changes to the positioning and spacing of the bearings within the strut and their lubrication.

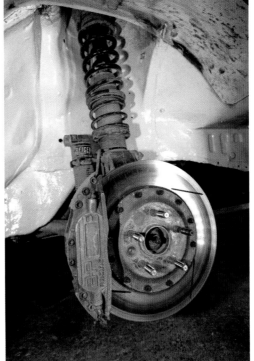

FAR LEFT The upper mounting point for the front suspension strut. *(Adam Warner)*

LEFT Easy access to the suspension is vital for making quick set-up changes and repairs. *(Adam Warner)*

The latter was achieved by the use of an oil circulation system. This worked by employing the pumping of the damper itself to keep circulating the oil from the bottom of the damper. There was an external pipe that ran from the bottom of the damper to above the top bearing so that as the car was driving down the road it kept pumping the oil around, creating a constant flow of oil over the bearings. This had the desired effect of making a significant improvement in reducing the amount of friction in the damper.

'You have a much stronger wall damper tube than you would on a normal road car, so there would be a machined tube with the ears welded on, which was then bolted to the upright,' Moreton explains. 'What we found was that with all the dust and the dirt that would get in between the bearings, the dampers would start to stick in the damper tubes. So we did a lot of work on the top seal to make sure that was right and then we developed a little oil pump system and a little one-way valve, so in the bottom of the damper it had 15mm of oil – just ordinary engine oil – a little one-way valve and a little Aeroquip fitting that had a hole between the two bearings where the damper tube ran up and down.'

In this new system, when the suspension was under compression it squashed the oil into the one-way valve and circulated oil around the damper – so it went from the bottom of the damper, through the one-way valve, so

that there was a shot of oil between the two bearings. Before this system was in place the team had to apply grease to a nipple situated between the two bearings at each service park. This was a time-consuming process. The self-lubricating pieces came along in time for the Impreza's debut at the 1000 Lakes in 1993. The

LEFT Many of the cars currently in action have had the original fixed dampers replaced with adjustable ones. *(Adam Warner)*

LEFT The detail work around the front anti-roll bar shows the simplicity of the Impreza design. *(Adam Warner)*

reduced friction meant that the dampers had to be recalibrated, so the benefits were instant and tangible.

Prodrive used Bilstein shock absorbers, with two versions generally available to each driver at the rallies. These were not adjustable items, so in order to made a comprehensive set-up change the team would have to swap out the damper units in the service park.

The fine-tuning of the suspension took place in testing, which is where the drivers had the opportunity to try various rates available and work out which ones worked best for them in the prevailing conditions. 'We used to have trays of them in the truck, all stamped which one was which, what rates they were,' Moreton recalls. 'We'd have probably four or six of each rate and they were different lengths front and rear. So there would be these lists of cabinets in the truck with these rows of dampers and we'd work through those and we'd start to arrive at a fairly reasonable setting.'

To change a damper rate the car needs to be jacked up so that the wheel can be taken off. Then there is free access to the damper unit, which bolts to the upright and to the turret at the top. This unit has got a spring on it that needs to be removed before it can be taken out and the actual damper, complete with the piston assembly for the oil system, removed. The damper can then be swapped out and in. Once the unit is back in place and the spring attached, the ride height needs to be reset and the wheel reattached. In a competitive environment, Prodrive could complete the whole procedure in a little more than ten minutes.

'On the test team we would have at least six to eight technicians,' says Moreton. 'A person per corner, somebody at the front and somebody on the jacks, so it was like a full service point. We weren't short of labour because I had this thing where it costs a lot of money to be away testing with hotels etc and the drivers' time is valuable. So at a test, by the time we had included the doctor – and you'd have Pirelli there with four or five people, and at least two engineers – so before you knew where you were we'd got 18 people. We always used to take two cars in case somebody crashed one, which used to happen now and again. A couple of times cars were

wrecked before we even started. Kenneth Eriksson scrapped one in Greece before we'd even started and Colin McRae did the same in another place where we were testing – we hadn't even got the base tyres on and they'd rolled them into a ball.'

Because of the forces that a rally car is subject to, from a wide array of different angles, ensuring the robustness of the suspension is vital. This is why the MacPherson strut is often the preferred solution. It's a surprisingly old design, with General Motors having filed the original patent in 1947. The strut is named after its inventor, Earle S. MacPherson, who was GM's chief engineer of its post-war Light Car project. It was the need to create a suspension that was light, small and strong that led him to create the MacPherson strut.

It's a very clever piece of design, which in its basic form uses a wishbone as a bottom mounting point for the axle or hub carrier of the wheel. This lower arm system provides both lateral and longitudinal location of the wheel. The upper part of the hub carrier is rigidly fixed to the bottom of the outer part of the strut itself. The line from the strut's top mount to the bottom ball joint on the control arm gives the steering axis inclination.

The strut usually carries both the coil spring on which the body is suspended and the shock absorber, which is usually in the form of a coilover. The strut can also have the steering arm built into the lower outer portion. The whole assembly is very simple and can be preassembled into a unit; also, by eliminating the upper control arm it allows for more width in the engine compartment, which is useful for a car like the Impreza and the wide design of its boxer engine. In the Impreza, the anti-roll bar replaces the radius arm at the bottom of the strut.

The amount of travel and stiffness was dependent on the surface, with the car lowest and stiffest on asphalt and softer with greater ground clearance on gravel. The snow set-up would be somewhere in the middle of these.

'The car always used to have the same amount of overall suspension travel,' says Moreton. 'About 210mm on the rear and 190mm on the front. It's heavier at the front and you're a bit more limited by the driveshafts. With the steering at the front you were constrained

by what you could get out of the driveshafts, because it wasn't only going up and down – you'd got it on a lock, so 190 was the maximum we could get out of it. We sometimes used to not bother with all the rebound travel on a tarmac car, but then on gravel you would be trying to sit in the middle of the suspension travel, whereas on tarmac you could be 50mm lower and you'd be working in the bottom third of the travel. Or somewhere like Kenya or the rough stages in Greece we'd be a bit more on tiptoes.'

Prodrive did have some special, extra-long dampers that it used in the Safari. These helped to raise the car up by 20mm all round in an effort to help it deal with the roughest and most unpredictable surface on the calendar.

Constant fine-tuning aside, there were no other major changes to the suspension in the Group A era, but Prodrive did take advantage of the freer WRC regulations to really push the technological envelope, even if it did turn out to be a dead end.

'We did do an electronic damper, but it was banned,' Lapworth laments. 'It did one rally and was banned. Prior to that we had developed an active damper. It was called DDV, which is the name of a valve. We had a valve in the lines of a remote canister that we were able to control at a high frequency with an ECU so that you could measure the speed and position of the damper and modify the curve of the damper.' Prodrive had first tested the system with McRae in

BELOW Prodrive developed a fully active car. It competed once – San Remo 2003 – before being banned. *(LAT)*

1998, but the one event the active car actually contested was the 2003 San Remo Rally with Petter Solberg.

'It was disappointing what happened,' Lapworth adds. 'The active suspension ran faultlessly, but there was a mistake in the code that meant the engine was down 30bhp for the whole rally and we couldn't find it. Petter spent the whole rally whinging that the car wasn't fast enough. The holy grail is a car that's soft yet stiff, and the active car was that. We ran the softest springs and the softest dampers ever run by miles and there was no roll and no pitch, so it was fast around the corners and brilliant under braking.'

Brakes

The sheer variety of corner types on rally stages makes secure and consistent braking a must. On the Group A Impreza, Prodrive partnered with brake specialists AP Racing. The size of brakes varied from surface to surface, with the biggest used on asphalt and the smallest on gravel, which is also in line with the size of tyres and wheels.

Although carbon brakes have long been de rigueur on track-racing cars, they never went past the conceptual stage in rallying before being outlawed on the basis of cost. 'They were banned before they made it on to the agenda,' confirms Lapworth. 'There are challenges in rallying and we never really understood whether they would have been beneficial or not. We were concerned about what happens when you drive through water, how quickly can you get them up to temperature, what happens when you throw mud at them, and I don't know, because we never answered those questions.'

In general, the brakes are as big as the wheel permits. The calliper is as large as the space available between the disc and the wheel. The front discs were 366mm on asphalt, 330mm on snow and 304mm on gravel. The rear discs were 304mm on all surfaces. Six-pot callipers were used on asphalt at the front, while four-pot were in situ on the rear throughout and on the front on snow and gravel.

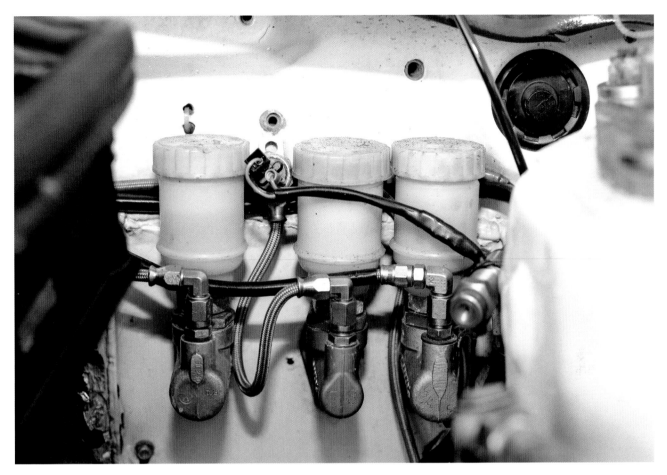

The benefit of running big brake discs is the greater surface area. The bigger the disc, the more heat it can disperse. This is important, because the key to reliable and effective braking is keeping the brakes at the correct temperature. If the brakes get too hot the surface of the pads can start melting, a process known as glazing. This makes the pads smooth and reduces friction between the pad and rotor. Also, if the calliper gets too hot it can cause the brake fluid to boil. If the fluid boils it gets bubbles in it, and bubbles in the system can mean the brake is flat to the floor without any actual braking taking place. Finally, even though the iron discs can handle temperatures of up to 600°C, if they overheat they can warp or even crack, which results in a catastrophic brake failure.

Although the braking system wasn't an area of enormous development during the Group A era, there was one key upgrade that took place, and that was the introduction of water-cooled front callipers.

'We were the first team to run water-cooled brakes,' Lapworth states. 'That was an

ABOVE **The master cylinders and reservoirs for the brake and clutch fluid.** *(Adam Warner)*

LEFT **AP supplied the brakes for the Group A Impreza.** *(Adam Warner)*

innovation we did with AP. There was a pump circulating water through the front callipers. There was a little radiator and a little pump – it was the intercooler pump from the Legacy, because that had a water-cooled intercooler. We had a little radiator and a little tank, just for the fronts. Rear brakes are a problem as it's not easy to force the air into them. Seventy-odd per cent of the braking on asphalt is at the front. We started off with a hand-made system with a bit of help from AP, which AP then developed into a proper cast-in water-cooled calliper.'

The water-cooled brake callipers ran to a max of 160°C. This ensured the brake fluid didn't boil on cars being driven by left-foot brakers and on rally sections involving mountain descents etc. Without the water-cooling, callipers could be reaching temperatures in excess of 200°C. And that was on the limit for brake fluid used in the 1990s. Another consequence of running at such high temperatures was that the piston seals deteriorated around this temperature range. Using the water-cooling also increased pad wear life because the whole brake package ran cooler without using increased brake cooling ducts.

The water pump was run constantly, but operated by a brake pedal switch and a time delay. The water coolant also included an inhibitor. Other than that the callipers would have a normal service interval for a competition car, which depended on how it was used. Water-cooling definitely increased the service intervals fairly substantially because they reduced running temperatures by around 25%, and that in turn reduced fluid boil and increased calliper piston seal life.

AP Racing's AP600 high-performance brake fluid was used at the time because of its ability to operate at high temperatures, and it's still available today. However, because it does not mix with other fluids the braking system needed to be drained completely and purged prior to final bleeding.

Along with the accelerator and clutch, the brake pedal was part of a pendulum set that hung off the front bulkhead. The handbrake was hydraulic, and was fitted with an electric switch that controlled the central diff, switching it off when a handbrake turn was required and back on again when the car was driving normally.

Engine

One of the areas of the Impreza that underwent the most development over the course of the Group A era was the engine. When Prodrive started the Legacy project the engines were built by Subaru in Japan. However, after a series of failures, not to mention a clear power deficit to its rivals, responsibility for engine development eventually switched to Banbury.

'It started off 100% Japan and it was very challenging, because the people there, whilst knowing a lot about road engines, knew nothing about motorsport,' says Lapworth.

'So the first couple of years with Legacy were unbelievably painful for both sides – the relationship was tense.'

But by the time the Impreza project was under way the engines were being built by Prodrive in the UK, while the long-term R&D was taking place at STi in Japan.

'At the end of the day they had to make the production parts and they had much better facilities than us to do proper measurement and endurance testing, and lots of sophisticated equipment that they had access to that we didn't,' adds Lapworth. 'So they would do a lot of the long-term research and they would do a lot of the fine-tuning. The mapping and the engine build we did in Banbury.'

Group A regulations were a complicated mix, mandating that elements such as the water pumps and valve sizes had to be the same as the road car version, but allowing almost total freedom on components such as camshafts. As a result some of the development that took place in the road car department was

BELOW Packaging a flat-four, boxer engine was one of the great challenges.
(Adam Warner)

influenced by the needs of the rally programme.

'It's difficult for us to know how much influence we were actually having,' recalls Lapworth. 'For sure, from the early days of the Legacy programme we'd identified a couple of things. The turbocharger was too small, and the intercooler not effective enough.

'The Legacy was definitely held back by intake temperatures and the turbocharger. We were running 25,000rpm turbo speeds on the Legacy and blowing turbos up like they were going out of fashion! We were struggling to saturate the restrictor. The restrictor wasn't the performance limit on the Legacy, it was the turbo blowing itself to pieces. With the intercooler on the Legacy we struggled to maintain air charge temperature beneath 60° and we needed a bigger intercooler, and the Impreza came with a bigger air-to-air intercooler on top of the engine underneath the scoop. It wasn't fantastic, but it was a big improvement over what we had in the Legacy. I think we had some influence in that but it's difficult to directly trace cause and effect.'

If you were watching at a rally stage in period, you could tell an Impreza was on its way long before it arrived. This was due to the distinctive burble of the engine, which was a product of its unique configuration. Unlike its rivals from Ford, Mitsubishi and Toyota, Subaru employed a flat-four 'boxer' engine rather than the more conventional inline four.

Subaru first started selling road cars with the boxer engine in 1966, and, along with four-wheel drive, it became part of the company's key differentiators. Subaru's first boxer engine was codenamed the EA, but this was phased out in 1989 and replaced by the EJ, which was fitted to both the Legacy and the Impreza and is still in use today. The EJ had an aluminium block with dry cast iron sleeves inside. It was available in single and double overhead cam versions and was fuel injected. It came in both normally aspirated and turbocharged forms, and ranged in size from 1.5 to 2.5 litres.

It was the 2-litre turbo EJ20 that formed the basis of all Subaru's rally engines from the start of the Legacy programme in 1990 until it withdrew from the sport at the end of 2008. That unit featured a bore and stroke of 92 x 75, ran a compression ratio of 8.8:1 and had a total capacity of 1,994.3cc. It had belt-driven double overhead camshafts and four valves per cylinder. The valves were coil-spring operated. The inlet valve was 36.2mm in diameter while the exhaust was 32.2mm. The engine was water-cooled, with a 7.7-litre capacity, and had a wet-sump lubricating system with a single oil cooler.

In theory the boxer engine design is better balanced and smoother than an inline four. This is because in an inline four the pistons are moving faster at the top half of the crank rotation than at the bottom, which causes the engine to vibrate up and down, and is the main reason that inline fours are seldom larger than 2 litres in capacity, as this problem is exacerbated by increased weight and piston speed. But in a boxer engine, because the pistons cannot be directly opposed, they have to be slightly offset. While this removes the imbalances of the inline four it does cause a rocking motion, which is one of the reasons such engines no longer have mainstream popularity.

The unique sound is a product of the firing order, which in the Impreza is 1, 3, 2, 4, or left-left-right-right if you're looking down on the engine with the bonnet up. This creates an irregular pulse spacing of the air into the intakes and exhaust gases into the manifold, and thus that distinctive burbling noise.

Motoring pioneer Karl Benz had designed the first boxer engine in 1897, the type getting its 'boxer' nickname from the layout of the pistons, which are horizontally opposed and move back and forth at the same time, making them look like boxers tapping gloves at the beginning of a fight.

It took just three years for Benz's 'contra engine', as it was called at the time, to be deployed in a motorsport environment, but it was in air-cooled form in the back on the Volkswagen Beetle that the flat-four found its calling, and designer Ferdinand Porsche would carry the engine concept over to the first of the cars to bear his own name. Indeed, Porsche is still using flat four- and six-cylinder engines in its cars to this day. However, Porsche and Subaru are pretty much alone in this respect, and there are some very good reasons for that.

'The disadvantage is that it's a bit heavy,' says Lapworth. 'The complexity of having two cylinders on one side, two cylinder heads, four camshafts, is huge. So despite being a pretty well-designed aluminium block and heads and so on, I think it's fair to say it was always heavier than the equivalent straight-four. Maybe 20 kilos, so a decent chunk.'

The boxer layout also creates a very square engine that, while potentially beneficial for lowering the centre of gravity, presents some very significant issues in terms of its placement and installation.

'It's quite a long way forward, because it has to sit ahead of the front diff,' adds Lapworth. 'You have the diff at the front of the gearbox with the cluster laid out behind it. In front of the front diff you have the clutch housing and the clutch and only at that point does the engine start. So you are quite a long way forward. In the equivalent transverse engine, the clutch is across the car. The Subaru was the only longitudinal engine (with the exception of the Escort Cosworth), so fore-and-aft weight distribution was probably not quite so good. So you do end up with a bit of work to try to get that back.'

Having the cylinders 180° apart also presents further problems with the design of the exhausts. It might make it sound great, but it makes situating all the externals such as the

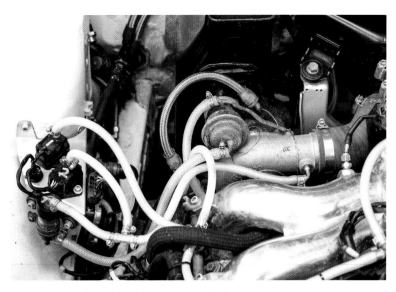

turbo, intercooler and exhausts a real challenge, and in some cases a bit of a compromise.

'With the exhaust system you are limited in what you can do because you can't get the turbocharger close to the exhaust ports, because they are underneath the engine,' Lapworth explains. 'The turbo sits on the top to the rear on the right-hand side looking in the driver's direction. So you imagine how far it is away from cylinder number one on the left front, and anybody who's developed a turbo engine will tell you that you want it close.

ABOVE The maze of tubing that feeds into the turbo wastegate. *(Adam Warner)*

LEFT The WRC rules allowed Prodrive to move the engine back and down in the engine bay. *(Prodrive)*

placement of the exhaust manifolds. To take advantage of the boxer design, the ideal is to get the engine as low as possible in the car, but this reduces the amount of space between the engine and the sump guard, limiting the options for the positioning of the manifold, which in turn can compromise the performance of the turbo.

A further complication arises from having the cylinders spread so far apart, and that's the positioning of the inlet manifolds. Rather than having a single inlet as is the case on an inline four, there has to be one on one side for the bank of two, and one on the other. 'For a single turbo you need some sort of plenum, and you have some problems with making all that work as nicely as you can,' Lapworth adds. 'Generally speaking you'd have shorter runners in a classic inline four.'

There are yet further complications inherent in an aluminium boxer design. Making the camshafts perform at a competition level, for instance. Because they have to be so far apart there is a long belt linking them, which with the heat expansion and contraction of the aluminium engine makes it a real challenge to maintain the torsion. Modern technology has all but solved these issues now with sophisticated tensioning systems, but in the early 1990s there was the real danger of the tensioners going lose and the belt jumping teeth.

ABOVE Even in a picture you can almost hear that distinctive burble from the exhaust. *(Adam Warner)*

'The exhaust system is also compromised, because you can't get the lengths of the primaries the same, which is normally a target – it's not an absolute law, but normally you have an optimum target length and you try to mix the bunch of bananas around so that they all end up the same length; and because you have an aluminium engine that's growing and shrinking and a massive exhaust system, and the bigger the exhaust system the more it grows and shrinks with temperature.'

This creates further issues with the

RIGHT The challenge of having the cylinders so far apart becomes apparent in this image. *(Adam Warner)*

LEFT Radiator plumbing and massive air intake hose. *(Adam Warner)*

'It was quite a challenge with the Subaru engine, because the change in belt tension was quite massive,' Lapworth says. 'And sorting that out with the lightweight flywheel and semi-automatic gearbox in particular, you start to introduce problems with belts jumping and pulley failures, and we had quite a lot of those in the 1997 era in particular.'

So clearly there were a multitude of issues to overcome if the engine was going to allow Subaru to fight for rally wins. But initially there was an even more pressing concern in the early days of the Legacy: reliability.

After a series of failures in 1990 and 1991, Prodrive brought the engine development in-house for 1992. However, at the time the company didn't have a dynamometer, so had to use nearby specialists in Cowley and Southam. The initial work was carried out by Graham Moore, who told David Williams in his book *The Rallying Imprezas* how they set about making the boxer a more reliable and competitive proposition.

'We did away with the head gasket. That helped us in a few other areas as well and that seemed to make the engine fairly bomb-proof after that. A couple of drivers did test it without any water in it for a few kilometres. It wasn't completely indestructible. You could get away with quite a few – so long as it had oil in. If you lost the oil, forget it, but if the oil was still in and the cooler was still working, 200 degree oil temperature, I've seen them recover, which is pretty amazing.'

When the Impreza came on line it brought with it a revised version of the EJ20 engine, which featured new cylinder heads, a bigger turbo and a revised cooling system, although the radiator was always the standard road car component from the WRX.

In the cylinder heads the valve angle had been reduced from 26° to 20.5°, and more conventional tappets had been fitted in place of the finger-type ones that had been a reliability concern on the Legacy, and there was a new overhead camshaft that operated directly on to

BELOW Additional coolant capacity is essential in a competition car. *(Adam Warner)*

cam followers in order to reduce the number of moving parts and improve reliability. But it was the larger IHI turbo and air-to-air intercooler that made the big difference and meant that Prodrive could start to claw back the power deficit that had been estimated at as much as 100bhp in the Legacy.

'One of the so-called advantages of a boxer engine is the ability to use a large bore short-stroke engine, and traditionally you'd say that was a good thing. And certainly with a normally aspirated engine it is good, but it's not so good when you're running a highly turbocharged engine,' says Lapworth. 'You want a better combustion chamber shape. The limitations of a restricted engine, especially a turbocharged engine, are thermodynamic, not mechanical. It's much better to have a small, compact combustion chamber than this very flat pancake that you end up with in a large-bore engine.

'Detonation in simple terms is the limiting factor. The world changes when you introduce direct injection, knock control etc, but if you ask any engineer for the ideal bore and stroke of a 2-litre turbocharged engine, he wouldn't come back and say "a 92mm bore". It would be in the 80s. I think it's OK to say that the bore and stroke were probably sub-optimal for a 2-litre turbocharged engine at the state of tune you are looking for in the World Rally Championship.

For a road car it's fine, at those levels of boost, and Subarus rev on quite nicely. There aren't many 2-litre engines that are comfortable at 8,000rpm on a road, but Subarus are. In a road car it's not a bad compromise, but when it comes to getting max power out of it at 5,500–6,000rpm it's not the right bore/stroke ratio.'

Subaru was given a helping hand ahead of the 1995 season when, unexpectedly, the FIA reduced the turbo intake restrictor from 38mm to 34mm. This resulted in a power loss of around 20%, or approximately 50bhp. But given that the engine had never really had the most power its overall loss was less, and, coupled with a new design of camshafts so that the engine worked more effectively at a lower rev range, the team was probably as close to parity with its rivals as it had ever been.

Nevertheless, some significant changes were required. The camshaft was re-profiled, the compression ratio was altered and the ECU software was updated as the team made significant gains in terms of anti-lag. Perhaps the area where the biggest changes were taking place in engine development in the early 1990s was in engine management technology. Electronic control units had started to appear in the 1980s along with the arrival of electronic fuel injection. But these were far away from the versions used in today's cars, where an

RIGHT No fly-by-wire here – the mechanical throttle linkage.
(Adam Warner)

engineer on a laptop can make a raft of changes in a single keystroke. Back in 1993 the engine management instructions were hardcoded and burned on to an EPROM (erasable programmable read-only memory) chip.

Each individual instruction had to be directly burned on to the chip. If there was a mistake, you had to take it out and start again. It was a potentially enormously time-consuming job, but in Matsurai Kurihara STi found someone who not only had a profound knowledge of the programme skills involved, but had a motorsport brain and understood Prodrive's requirements.

'Kurihara is very clever and understood electronics and maths and was a proper academic, but with a real good feeling for motorsport,' says Lapworth. 'Although he wasn't a motorsport man, he kind of got it. But he was regarded as a bit of an outcast by the Japanese, and it was always a rather strange relationship. But we got on really well with him. We would say, "Can you do this?" and he would say "Yes, I can." And that was a really good balance. We understood the motorsport application, we could guess what software, what algorithms we were looking for, but he was brilliant at taking them away and coming back and saying, "Try that bit of code."

'We made massive strides and we moved very quickly, because he was prepared to be a maverick by Japanese standards and say, "Yeah, that's a really good idea, I could do some code for that," and we rapidly went through anti-lag and boost control and knock control and closed-loop lambda and all those things that are taken for granted these days but couldn't be taken for granted then. We worked through that menu pretty quickly and efficiently with his help and we probably couldn't have done it without him, and we could point him in the right direction and let him loose.'

Getting to grips with engine management meant that not only were the engines more powerful, more reliable and more drivable, it also gave rise to the possibility of introducing driver aids such as launch and traction control. Initially these systems were pretty agricultural, but they did allow for some rather spectacular performances off the line.

'We used to call it the dial-on accident!' Lapworth jokes.

The system worked by placing a brake balance bar on a throttle stop, which allowed the driver to wind the brake balance forward. The software would keep the engine at launch speed – roughly 2,500rpm. Then, with the brakes on hard, the driver had to dial up the turbo to something like 60,000rpm, for which there was a small read-out on the dashboard display. With the car shaking under the pent-up forces, the driver would then let the brake off and unleash the fury.

'It was always a bit hit and miss, and if you overdid it you'd get a bit of push going into the corners,' Lapworth recalls, 'but there was a limit to how much we could retard and cut, so it would sometimes push on a little bit in a hairpin, which was OK after you got used to it and factored it in – the brakes get a bit hot – but it is a bit scary if you've never experienced anything like it before. I remember Carlos raising his eyebrows and saying, "Are you sure? Maybe let's go a bit lower…".'

Since the introduction of turbocharging into motorsport in the late 1970s one of the biggest challenges all the manufacturers faced was reducing and, ideally, eliminating turbo lag. Turbo lag is caused by the time it takes the turbo to spool up and deliver its induction boost.

In many cases the solution was to employ a twin turbo set-up, with the smaller turbo designed to function at low revs and the larger one kicking in higher up the rev range. However, with just a single turbo to play with this wasn't an option for Prodrive and Subaru.

The turbo fitted to the Impreza was the IHI VF15 RHB52. It featured a steel turbine of 58mm diameter and an aluminium compressor with a 65mm diameter. Between 1993 and 1994 it ran with a 38mm restrictor as mandated by the FIA, but for 1995 and 1996 this was reduced to 34mm. As also dictated by the rules a catalytic convertor was fitted. This was Bosch's L-jetronic multi-point electronic fuel injection system, developed back in the 1960s. By the mid-1990s the air-pressured control system was refined to the point where off-the-shelf units were suitable for the requirements of motorsport if mated to the correctly programmed ECU.

The size of the turbo was the biggest change from the Legacy engine to the Impreza, and with the Group A rules requiring the rally version to employ the same size of turbo as the road version this was a huge boost in terms of overcoming the power deficit.

'The turbo was one area where we were happy to have solid, conservative Japanese engineering,' says Lapworth. 'Japan dealt with them, and politically they wanted IHI. We could have gone for Garret or something, but they wanted IHI, which is a close partner of Subaru.'

In an era of unlimited turbo boost – with some manufacturers running upwards of 3.5 bar – ensuring the turbos ran as efficiently as possible was of primary concern.

'I think we led the way, to be fair,' adds Lapworth. 'I suspect we were one of the first people to run rolling element bearings in turbochargers at a high level efficiently. The boost efficiency, free-running and reliability were excellent. There was no boost limit. It got ridiculous, sort of 3.5 bar boost, but just because you can doesn't mean you should. There is a limit to how wide the power band needs to be and when it's wide enough you should concentrate on making it higher, but just because you can run ludicrous amounts of boost at a lower rpm doesn't mean you should.'

The boost battle really reached a head in the WRC era that followed on from Group A in 1997. During the preceding period, the main focus was on developing anti-lag systems.

'We were running quite high levels of boost and we were making rapid progress through that era with anti-lag. One of the highlights of the '94/'95/'96 period was a rapid development in anti-lag,' Lapworth recalls. 'That's a classic example of matching our practical experience with Kurihara's willingness to develop software.

'We had anti-lag at a low level on the very first Legacy in 1989. We simply jacked the throttle open and retarded the ignition at idle until we raised the background turbocharger speed. We were quite conservative, because we didn't know what the limits were and we didn't have proper turbo speed management at the time, and we didn't know how we were going to get on with the durability of exhaust systems and all the rest.'

Prodrive didn't have a dedicated test driver at the time, so a lot of the early shakedown work used to be conducted by Lapworth himself, often at the MIRA test facility that's about 40 miles away near Nuneaton. With no

prior knowledge of how the system would work, Lapworth and his team embarked on a process of trial and error, retarding the ignition a little bit more each time.

'After each one I could start to feel something and it was starting to pick up, but not what you would recognise as full anti-lag,' he says. 'We went as far as you can achieve with retard, not going into cylinder cuts because we didn't have the software. We probably went 20% of the journey that we later did by simply opening the throttle and retarding the ignition. You could detect a bit of a difference.'

But the seed had been sown, so the aim for the Impreza programme was to have full anti-lag, which they were able to achieve thanks to Kurihara's ECU programming skills.

Cool air aids the combustion process and is crucial for turbo engines to operate effectively. The change of intercooler from water to air, as used in the Legacy, to air to air in the Impreza also played a key role in boosting the engine performance. An air-to-air intercooler uses the air that is flowing into the intercooler to cool the air in the charge pipes. Therefore the position of the air-to-air intercooler is vital. In a water-to-air intercooler water is pumped through it, where it cools the air in the charge pipes. The mounting position is almost irrelevant but it does require a water pump, reservoir and a heat exchanger.

The benefit of the air-to-air intercooler is that it requires no external parts, so is lighter, but it can be difficult to situate and is only as effective as the air that is going into it.

ABOVE The placement of the turbo and its plumbing was a challenge. *(Adam Warner)*

LEFT The bonnet scoop that forces air into the intercooler. *(Adam Warner)*

BELOW LEFT Radiator air intake at the bottom, turbo intercooler at the top. *(Adam Warner)*

BELOW The air-to-air intercooler that was introduced on the Impreza. *(Adam Warner)*

97

Fuel system

The Impreza ran on high-performance turbo race fuel, normally rated at 104 Ron. To deal with this more combustible fuel the whole system was bespoke, from the fuel rails to the Aeroquip fuel lines. The 75-litre fuel tank is situated in the boot inside a protective casing.

Gearbox

Together with its nimble handling, one of the Impreza's greatest strengths was its sweet and slick gearchange. Group A rules allowed almost total freedom in the gearbox, and Prodrive took full advantage of this to introduce its own design, which was based on the tried and tested concept it had used on the BMW M3 project that preceded its involvement with Subaru. However, they didn't plan to stick with this six-speed, H-pattern 'box. In fact, at the programme's inception the target was to develop and introduce a semi-automatic gearbox.

ABOVE **75-litre fuel tank located behind the spare wheel.** *(Adam Warner)*

BELOW **The well-drilled mechanics can strip a car in minutes.** *(Prodrive)*

After a period of research and development the decision was taken to go down the pneumatic system route, based on the sound logic that you never run out of air, and that this system offered a degree of compliance.

In 1989, when work on the Legacy programme began, Ferrari had been the first team in Formula 1 to introduce a semi-automatic gearbox. This meant that no off-the-shelf options were available, so Prodrive had to set about developing its own system from scratch. However, in the conceptualisation stage they made a fundamental error, as Lapworth explains:

'The mistake we made, with the benefit of hindsight, was that we thought we could automate the H-pattern. Of all the options available – sequential and H-gate, air and hydraulic – we didn't get the right two first time around. If we'd done a sequential air system, history shows that 50% or more of the race cars out there these days – including Aston Martins – actually have a pneumatic system working perfectly well. And we also later proved that we could run an hydraulic system following the H-pattern, which had some advantages. Basically it has quicker shifts than you could achieve with a sequential system because the sequential system has a lot of inbuilt friction in it, which limits the amount of load you can put on the shift mechanism.'

But this knowledge was only apparent in hindsight, and in period Prodrive ploughed on with the development of its pneumatic H-pattern gearbox. In fact, it was even homologated and fitted to the cars, but the drivers were instructed to disengage the system and it was only ever used on the road sections between stages. The main issue was that the system was never fully reliable and barely quicker than the standard manual system, while the feedback from the drivers was less than complimentary too.

The system worked in a similar way to John Barnard's system in the Ferrari 640, by means of a paddle behind the steering wheel. As well as making the gearchanges theoretically faster, the system also meant the drivers could keep both hands on the wheel, making the car easier to drive, and, if the H-pattern stick shifter had been removed, improved the cabin ergonomics. But none of these benefits were enough to justify the risk, so instead the drivers simply flicked a switch, depressurised the system and drove as they normally would. However, there was a key benefit to keeping the system on the car…

'We took advantage of some loopholes in the homologation regulations, which we can talk about now, which was that automatic gearboxes were allowed a different flywheel,' admits Lapworth. 'When everybody else was running their Group A heavy flywheel we had a nice lightweight racing flywheel homologated for the automatic gearbox. So for a couple of years we ran with a nice lightweight flywheel off the back of having an automatic gearbox, which was not being used but gave us a useful performance advantage.'

Eventually the decision was made that they had simply backed the wrong horse with the pneumatic H-gate system, and the decision was made to explore the hydraulic route, which the road racing side of the company had developed successfully for the touring car

BELOW **The Group A Imprezas featured an H-pattern gearbox.** *(Adam Warner)*

ABOVE **By 2004 Prodrive had introduced a full semi-automatic gearbox, with steering-mounted paddle shifts.** *(Prodrive)*

programme. However, by the time this system was rally-ready Group A had ended and the WRC cars has been introduced.

'If we'd known the journey we were taking we wouldn't have bothered with the pneumatic – we'd have gone with the sequential first, and we'd probably have ended up with pneumatic then. But we learnt a lot from the hydraulic approach and I believe we achieved a faster, better shift with the hydraulic system than we did with the sequential,' says Lapworth.

The gearbox used internals from Hewland and was designed by Bob Farley and John Piper. It always contained six speeds regardless of the rally surface, despite some of its rivals running five, or even four-speed versions on occasion.

Because of the demands of the rally, the power of the engine and, in some cases, the lack of mechanical sympathy from the drivers, the gearbox would usually be changed at least once over the course of a rally. Prodrive had the capability to rebuild a gearbox overnight in the service park, with the most common issue being drivers rounding the dogs off.

'Colin was brilliant, Carlos wasn't too bad, some others who I won't name couldn't do a rally without rounding the dogs off, and it tended to be inversely proportional to their speed,' Lapworth states.

In order to help them learn how to treat the car a little more kindly, he would suggest they went out for a passenger ride with Colin or Carlos. A lot of drivers were resistant to this, but

once they'd overcome their reluctance – and in some cases fear – they were usually intrigued to discover that with speed came smoothness, and with smoothness came a more sympathetic treatment of the gearbox.

While the F1 teams were starting to explore the idea of carbon fibre gearbox casings at the time, the enormous cost of this approach was prohibitive, meaning magnesium replaced aluminium and was the go-to material at the time.

The same applies to the clutch. Carbon clutches became de rigueur by the mid-1990s, and over the course of its lifespan the Group A Impreza went from having a double-plate clutch in 1993 and '94 to a triple-plate cera-metallic clutch in 1995. Finally, a fully carbon version supplied by AP Racing was introduced in 1996.

The advantage of a carbon clutch is firstly weight, but also reliability. Prodrive were capable of an effective intermediate rebuild, checking the pressure plate etc, but for full rebuilds – which took place after every rally – they would go back to the supplier.

By the early 1990s the vast majority of rally drivers were left-foot braking and only really using the clutch at the start and following a handbrake turn. In the Subaru line-up, McRae was fully committed to left-foot braking, while Sainz would occasionally right-foot brake on asphalt in order to balance the car.

In the final season of Group A, 1994 World Champion Didier Auriol – out of a drive after Toyota was thrown out of the championship – did a one-off drive for the team and used his classic heel-and-toe right-foot braking technique, but by this point in time he was one of the very few still employing this method.

Differential

Alongside the aim for semi-automatic transmission, the other key mission that Prodrive set itself at the outset of the Legacy project was the development of fully active transmission. And unlike the gearbox development woes outlined previously, in the differential Prodrive finally attained its goals, via step-by-step iterations.

The journey started out with the aim of securing hydraulic control of the rear diff.

Initially the team lacked the confidence to introduce a full hydraulic version, so in the Legacy it adapted a conventional mechanical diff with an hydraulic overlay. This was carried over into the Impreza, but by now Prodrive had introduced a fully hydraulic centre diff, which was soon followed by a full hydraulic front diff and ultimately led to the addition of a hydraulic rear diff ahead of the 1995 season. The hydraulic diffs were then superseded by completely active versions when the WRC car came on line in 1997.

'We started with a conventional limited slip differential with ramps and plates,' explains Lapworth, 'and we have a device which we designed into it mechanically that is a response to the amount of torque that the diff is carrying. The torque that you can transmit – the torque difference across the differential – the amount of torque you can put to the outside wheel and the inside wheel, the difference between those – is a function of the ramp angle and the level of friction in the plates and so on, but it's designed in. You can change it, you can say, "OK, let's change a 45° ramp for a 30° ramp. Let's put a 30° ramp on the drive side and an 80° ramp on the overrun side. We'll go from six friction faces to 12 friction faces." You can play all those tunes but you get what you dial in.'

Taking this mechanical set-up and overlaying it with an hydraulic system adds a new level of adjustability. Using an hydraulic piston, working in parallel with the ramps and plates, Prodrive was able to add hydraulic pressure to that piston to increase the load on the diff. This meant that in practice a slightly lower target for the diff could be set, but that it was backed up with hydraulic pressure. This is known as an 'open loop map'.

In order to define these maps, the team had to embark on a detailed testing programme. The driver would have to go up and down in all the anticipated conditions, and establish the settings required at full throttle, half-throttle and so on, so that the correct amount of pressure could be mapped.

The next stage was to set a wheel-by-wheel speed target, which is where the benefit of the hydraulic system came into play. So rather than trying to measure pressures, the aim instead is to determine speed. This means that a target

slip percentage can be determined, and the system itself adjusts for the amount of pressure that is required to achieve this.

'If you look at the 1995 car you see that there is a percentage slip front diff pot that Colin could slide forward and dial in the amount of slip he wanted on the front diff and the same for the centre diff,' says Lapworth, 'and by the end of the era the rear diff as well. That gives the driver quite a lot of control over the way the car feels. That was the journey we took with the differentials.'

Through the rigorous testing programme, most of the work on the diff had been completed by mid-1995, although it wouldn't be until 1997 that all three diffs were made fully active. But at the beginning of the process it was a very intensive programme because they were asking questions to which the answers were genuinely unknown. They had an idea of what they were looking for, but needed the data to back up their hunches.

'We went to Corsica to do a tarmac test and we thought, "We're going to go through a plan – we're not going to try to optimise it right away, we're going to try to learn what the role of each of these diffs is and get an understanding of how aggressive you need to be," and so on,' Lapworth recalls. 'So the plan was to start to run the car with all the diffs switched off, so we tell Colin it's not going to be very good, but just learn the road and drive the car up and down and one by one we'll ramp them up and you'll

start to feel the role that each of them plays and the way the car works.

'So we start with the centre diff, which we knew from the previous work what we expected the setting to be, so we mapped that in. Then we did the rear diff and got the answer we expected, and then we did the front diff. But the starting point was fully locked; and just to see what he says with the three diffs locked – Colin's fastest time of the day was with three diffs locked! His comment was, "It's a bit tricky to drive. If you don't get it right it's not very forgiving, but if you do get it right and you stick to the racing line and turn in in the right place and get on the throttle when you need to, it's amazingly good." Which helps put things in perspective!'

That understanding is that while engineering has to be an academic exercise, and attention to the details is important, it's the bigger picture that's paramount. There are refinements and there are fundamentals. And once you understand the fundamentals, often the solution can be simple.

McRae was highly regarded as a test driver by the team, due to the clarity of his feedback. However, his patience was limited and once his interest had been lost it was pretty much game over. 'The first two hours of any test with Colin were the best,' says Lapworth. 'By lunchtime you might as well have sent him home. Unless

you had something really, really interesting he got bored.'

This short attention span could lead him into searching for shortcuts in the process that didn't really exist.

'When we came to doing the active rear diff we adopted the same philosophy as with the hydraulic test,' Lapworth recalls. 'We said, "Let's go through the basics again, starting with the rear diff locked and rear diff open and then introduce the first level of control and then mark two and three and so on." Again we thought we knew by this time, with three years of running active diffs, where we wanted to end up, but we thought we would go on the journey and make the big changes and see what we learn. Colin did about two or three runs, and said, "Can't we just go to the best map?" At the time it was hilarious – as if we knew what the best map was! "That's the whole point, Colin, we're trying to get there, and by the end of today we're hoping to put you in the right place."'

Despite McRae's keenness to cut to the chase, he was a key part of the test programme, as Prodrive didn't have a dedicated test driver. As mentioned previously, Lapworth would often conduct the initial test runs himself just to check that all the systems were working. For systems such as the differentials much of the testing took place on asphalt. The reason for this is that everything shows up on asphalt as you work through the various parts of the programme. If a car's not working, its shortfalls will be more apparent on asphalt than on gravel, which can be more forgiving. So for the process of weighing up change A versus change B, it makes more sense to hit the black stuff.

The fundamental principles that are explored during testing are stiffness, weight distribution and centre of gravity etc. Any flaws in any of these areas are quickly apparent on an asphalt stage. On gravel every run is different to the one before, so it's almost impossible to do a proper test on gravel because there are two things that are fundamentally unavoidable: one is that the road changes every time you drive on it – you cannot get two runs the same; the other is that this is rallying, not racing – the drivers need to drive it on pace notes so there's a level of improvisation, and if drivers have driven down the road twice they are no longer improvising.

Satisfied that the concept had been proved in testing, the active front diff was introduced ahead of the 1994 New Zealand Rally. It brought with it a small weight penalty of around eight kilos, but the performance increase was adjudged to be sufficient to overcome this.

Certainly McRae was convinced, as he is quoted in *The Rallying Imprezas* as saying: 'First of all the centre diff and then the active front diff made a big difference to the car. It just meant the car was more controllable in longer corners and bad cambers. The problem with the old mechanical diffs was that you could spin the car very easily. It would lift a front wheel and then you would have no drive at all, but if it lifts a front wheel with an active diff, you've still got the active part driving the wheel and it pulls the car again.'

Tyres

The single biggest change that took place between the 1993 RAC Rally and the Impreza's first appearance on the stages in 1994 was the switch from Michelin to Pirelli tyres.

Pirelli had worked with Prodrive before, supplying the tyres for its BMW programme in 1987. But for 1988 it had transferred its attention to the Toyota team, helping the Japanese manufacturer to secure its first-ever world title with Carlos Sainz in 1990, a

feat he repeated on the Italian rubber again in 1992. But with Toyota moving to Michelin for 1993, Pirelli spent a season on the sidelines. During that year discussions between Prodrive boss David Richards and Pirelli's then head of motorsport Dario Calzavara solidified into a deal that would ultimately cover the rest of Subaru's tenure in the World Rally Championship.

Following a handful of tests in 1993 the project was given the green light, and when Colin McRae and new Subaru signing Sainz took the ceremonial start in Monaco it was on Pirelli's tyres.

Being the only representative of a tyre manufacturer is a double-edged sword. On the plus side, Subaru was the company's sole focus; the tyres were developed for the specific needs of the car and preferences of its drivers. On the downside, when Michelin brought a better tyre Subaru and its drivers found themselves disadvantaged against the entire field, meaning that a relatively small performance shortfall could be exacerbated into something much worse in terms of the overall result.

The change of tyres didn't require any profound re-engineering of the car, just some adjustments to the cambers and pressures that were run. Other than those that were required by the demands of the particular rally, there were no overt changes to the spring rates or damping levels that the cars were set up with.

Pirelli used its relationship to not only develop and improve the performance of the cars, but to use that technology transfer to improve the products it sold to its road car customers. Initially this was an era of almost zero restrictions, with no limit on the amount of testing that could take place and huge amounts of freedom on the number of types of tyres that could be brought and used on a rally.

Tapping into the classical engineering approach practised by Lapworth and his team, Pirelli dedicated a lot of time and resources to the programme to ensure that it was at least on a par with the tyres that Michelin was developing.

The freedoms allowed by the regulations meant that Pirelli was producing something in the order of 10,000 tyres a season for Subaru alone! In the era before the central service parks were introduced in 1995 teams were free to change tyres after every stage, and this was an opportunity that they were not going to turn down. But this flexibility meant that Pirelli had to be prepared for almost every type of weather and road condition, meaning that literally scores of different compounds and tread types were brought along just in case they were needed.

By the end of the Group A era the teams were even employing their own weather forecasting crews who would helicopter further down the stages and report back on the conditions so that the correct tyres could be prepared for the stage to come. It was an impressive feat of organisation and logistics, if enormously expensive and ultimately unsustainable.

On top of the various compounds and treads, there were three basic types of tyre: tarmac, gravel and snow. These are three completely different types of tyre in terms of size, compound and construction. Pirelli's rally boss of the era, Fiorenzo Brivio, explains: 'There was a real tailored design according to the surface. Back then the rallies were changing

much more from year to year than they are now, so there were many factors that had to be taken into consideration: the length of the stage and the type of surface etc. But the giant step for us was the possibility to test new materials in the casing of the tyres and new materials in the tread compound, which in that era became more and more sophisticated. We were able to give a real impulse to tyre development because of the amount of testing we were able to do.

'One of the main differences in design of a rally tyre to a circuit tyre is that because a rally tyre has to deal with the grip of the road on tarmac and on gravel and all the other different surfaces like snow or ice in Monte Carlo, it's so inconsistent and is really difficult to replicate in a model; so far as I know there is still not a model that they can make in a virtual reality. A rally tyre has to be designed and produced before going into a final production stage, so testing is a crucial part. This means you are still forced to bring a number of different solutions to the testing environment and select them at that stage.'

BELOW Keeping the rims clean and tidy is a crucial job. *(Prodrive)*

Because of the almost limitless freedoms, Pirelli and Subaru embarked on extensive test programmes that took them all over the world. For example, in order to test the tyres ahead of the Safari Rally they would head to the outback in Australia, where it's possible to simulate the gruelling conditions in Kenya. Pirelli's test team was equipped with a container that had everything it needed for fitting and inflating the tyres, as well as a small office. With this up and running they could test pretty much anywhere around the world, although approximately 60% of the testing was on asphalt, with the majority of the remainder taking place on gravel and only a small amount on snow and ice. Prodrive and its contracted drivers were used for all of the tests, although some were more interested in the tyre development process than others.

'There are basically two kinds of drivers,' Brivio reckons. 'Ones with an engineering mentality who want to get inside how the tyres behave, how the tyre is made and how the compound is working, how the construction is reacting; and other drivers who depend much more on their own feelings. I'm not saying that they were not good, they could still tell you what felt good or bad.

'Carlos tried to understand better how to help the development of the tyre. On the other hand there are drivers likes Juha Kankkunen and Colin McRae who are more feeling-based. They were good and quite straight, they were experiencing the tyre and giving their impression in quite a clear way. Normally they were not going back and forth, they were quite consistent in their feedback.

'Colin was really very quick and in the end he didn't like to stay long in the car and think about making it faster. He was the kind of driver who goes fast from the off. He was a very instinctive driver.'

As a result of all this testing some key developments took place, with the introduction of run-flat mousse inserts being the most crucial. The threat of a puncture lurks around almost every corner for a rally driver, so creating a tyre that's effectively puncture-proof takes a huge load off of their mind, especially on gravel rallies littered with sharp and jagged rocks, like Cyprus or the Acropolis in Greece.

Pirelli started to develop its EMI (Espanso Modulare Integrato) tyre at the end of the 1992 season, a process it continued through 1993 before it was introduced in 1994. At first EMI was only available in the gravel tyres but it was eventually expanded to the asphalt rubber as well. Initially Pirelli developed the mousse system in-house, before finding a third-party supplier that was able to produce it in a more efficient way.

Brivio explains how the EMI system works: 'It's kind of a sponge, but with a sponge you can have two different types. You can have a sponge with open cells, which are the ones you normally use for washing your car, and this kind of sponge can absorb water or air or any kind of liquid you want to put in, because the cells are all connected to each other. But the EMI system is a mousse – a sponge with closed cells. The material is made with a rubber compound that is like an inner tube, like the ones they used to have in cars before tubeless tyres were introduced. This tube is made of a particular rubber compound called butyl, and the sponge sets with closed cells. The specific characteristic of butyl rubber is that it is not permeable to the air, so that when you have air inside those cells it doesn't easily get outside.'

All the cells inside the sponge have a latent pressure at the ambient temperature. These increase as the temperature rises during the rotation of the tyre and the movement of the mousse inside. So as the temperature increases the size of the insert increases, which in turn generates pressure on the tyre wall and the thread inside the tyre, particularly when the tyre is punctured.

So if a tyre is deflated, the internal temperature of the insert goes up much more because of the internal friction with the carcass. The internal volume increases much more and generates quite a lot of pressure to make the tyre as efficient as when it was inflated with air.

'If you had a big cut on the side of the tyre you could see the pressure of the mousse force the material outside of the tyre, because of the high pressure generated inside,' Brivio adds.

As a new technology – and one that could occasionally upset the balance of the car, especially over a long stage where the tyres would get particularly hot regardless of whether they had been cut – Pirelli was cautious in

ABOVE The Pirelli tyres are put to the test by McRae on the 1996 San Remo.
(Prodrive)

introducing the EMI system, which possibly gave its Michelin rivals a key advantage.

'Michelin were quicker off the mark with the mousse systems,' says Lapworth. 'Pirelli struggled to get on top of that. Eventually we got there, but it was a long journey, whereas with Michelin we'd already tested them with Alen in the early 1990s and they were already there. It was a big jump, and the consequences of that jump were significant on the development of the car and the tyre, because when you know that you don't have to worry about punctures you don't worry about punctures. That changes things.'

The construction of all the tyres, regardless of whether they featured the EMI system, was effectively radial, but with a belt and a criss-crossed ply too. However, there was one terrain where the mousse system was not suitable, and that was in the unpredictable challenge of the Safari Rally. High speeds and extreme heat meant the butyl mousse melted here, so Pirelli looked to the past for inspiration and the run-flat tyres it had developed for Toyota to win its first Safari in 1984.

Rather than the sidewall cuts that are the typical type of puncture on a gravel stage, on the Safari the most common cause of tyre failure is what's known as an impact puncture, basically hitting a rock or a pothole at full speed, causing a big compression on the sidewall. Under such circumstances run-flat tyres allow the driver to continue at a controlled speed without air in the tyre. Initially designed for the road, so that people could

continue their journey without having to stop in the middle of a motorway to fix a puncture, the technology became commonplace in rallying during the 1980s and remains so to this day.

Pirelli was also active in Formula 1 in the early 1990s, but there was no crossover of technology from one project to the other, even in the case of the sticky, slick asphalt tyres.

'Generally speaking rally tyre construction is much stronger and more stiff, not because of the puncture risk, which is much higher, but because of the high load that is generated by the weight of the car, the power and the relatively small size of the tyre,' explains Brivio. 'If you think of a single-seater car, they have a very big tyre compared to the weight and have a very low centre of gravity, so a relatively small load transfer in the corner; whereas in a rally car with a high centre of gravity and high load transfer, the tyre is small compared to the weight and size of the car.'

Still the physical and chemical process by which the tyre generates its grip on asphalt is the same. The aim is always to have as much rubber in contact with the surface as possible at all times. This is why asphalt tyres are the biggest and widest of all the tyres used in rallying. However, asphalt is also the most changeable of road surfaces. It can get hot, it can get cold and icy, it could be damp, it could be abrasive or it could be smooth and slippery.

All of these different scenarios require a different compound of tyre. The biggest factor in determining which will be the correct one is establishing the temperatures in which it will operate and finding a tyre that works best in that window. In the era of the Group A Impreza, deciding what tyre would be best suited to the job in hand came down to the relationship between the engineer that developed the tyre and the driver himself.

Because a lot of rally driving is based on confidence, it's essential that the driver feels that his input is important in making the final decision. The tyre engineer would offer an opinion and state the facts with regard to the options available, but ultimately the decision would be taken by the driver. Which, of course, removed one excuse in the event of them crashing.

One further option available to Pirelli and the Subaru drivers was cutting the tyres, which is a fine skill that has developed over the years. The cut itself is not created at the scene, but rather there are a number of different stencil options available matched to the particular conditions of the stage. Cutting a set of tyres takes around 20 minutes. The cutting machine works by heating a blade to a temperature where it literally cuts the rubber like butter. There is a pattern for each groove that is followed, each taking only a matter of seconds, but which has to be repeated multiple times across all four tyres.

The design of the tread of the tyre will cut through the surface layer – whether that's gravel, dirt or water – to make contact with the solid surface beneath. Development in the design of tyre treads is ongoing and never ending.

There was a single change to the tyre regulations during the Subaru Group A period, which came in for the 1995 season. This was the outlawing of full-on slicks, replacing them with moulded slicks with a minimum of a 17% tread pattern. During the Group A period, Pirelli started to work on an asymmetric tread design, an idea that was subsequently picked up by all its rivals. The asymmetric concept is the orientation of the blocks that are opposite to the direction of the stress. The benefit is the rigidity of the tread, so basically more performance and optimised tread wear.

Tested on the Group A car, but rallied on the WRC version in 1997, was Pirelli's new type of snow tyre. The snow tyre works very differently from its gravel and asphalt cousins. Rather than using a large footprint to maximise grip, this tyre is narrow to cut through the snow; and while the tread still gains grip from the compacted snow beneath it, it's the tungsten studs embedded in the tyre that create the real grip.

Following a disastrous Rally Sweden in 1994, where the studs fell out of the tyres, Pirelli set about improving the way they were bonded to the rubber. Their solution was a moulded stud. The studs were inserted during the fabrication of the tyre before the curing stage so that the bond between stud and compound was created by the chemical curing process. This made it very strong, much stronger than any other type of gluing system used previously.

An additional benefit was that the protrusion of the studs – the extension of the stud outside the tread – was very accurate. This was because of the mechanical control of the fabrication process. The bonding is made by a chemical system in which the studs are plated with a special material that creates a molecular link between the compounds and the metal surface. This design of snow tyre is still used by Pirelli today, not only in its rally tyres but also in the studded road tyres it sells in the Scandinavian road car market.

Over the full course of their relationship, Subaru and Pirelli claimed three drivers' championships. Over three seasons under Group A rules, they won the 1995 title with McRae as well as the manufacturers' title,

ABOVE Pirelli developed a snow tyre in which the studs were moulded into the rubber. *(Prodrive)*

BELOW Tyre selection is one of the most crucial decisions in rallying. *(Prodrive)*

ABOVE To cut through
the snow and ice, in
Sweden narrow tyres
are used. (Prodrive)

which they defended the following season.
So it was clearly a fruitful relationship.
However, it's impossible to know whether
Subaru would have enjoyed the same
amount of success, or even more, had it
stuck with Michelin after 1993.

'Strategically it's interesting to debate the
advantages and disadvantages of being on
the same tyre as everybody else,' Lapworth
argues. 'It's very difficult to say over the course
of the season – I think Pirelli would probably
accept that in the context of the whole WRC
championship in the 1990s, you probably would
have been better off on Michelin. They had a
more developed product, and their tyres were
more versatile.

'In their day, in the right circumstances, Pirelli
had some great tyres. They were particularly
good in wet, cold, slippery conditions, and if
you look at our history of winning Rally GB
you'll see it's dominated by Subaru and Pirelli,
and that is partly down to the fact that we had
Richard Burns and Colin McRae and Petter

Solberg, who were all very good at Rally GB,
but it's also down to Pirelli.

'And they had other tyres along the way
that were brilliant in the right circumstances.
Good in New Zealand, good in Greece if it
was dry and hard. There was the XR tyre, a
wide gravel tyre with a very mild tread pattern,
so it was half-decent on a clean line or even
on tarmac. So Pirelli had in their range a
number of tyres that were great. That meant
we were very strong on a number of rallies,
and of the 40-odd wins that Subaru had, on
a lot of them some of the credit should go
to Pirelli, because we were the only team on
Pirelli. When they got it right we pretty much
had it sewn up, and that is the benefit of being
on a different tyre.

'But would I change things if we could go
back? Probably not. I think it would be fairer
to blame the championships that we didn't
win and should have on other things than
the tyres. I suspect that over a season you
were a few points better off on Michelin, but

we certainly picked up some wins because of Pirelli, and I don't think the difference was enough to say that using Pirellis cost us any championships. It was the retirements that costs us those points.'

The freedom, intense development and determination to outdo each other meant that Michelin and Pirelli were involved in probably the greatest tyre war in rallying's history. It made it a brilliant period for the boffins in the labs and the engineers on the stages, but the sheer expense could have ultimately driven the sport into the ground.

Michelin is a bigger company than Pirelli and ultimately had more resources. But Pirelli had a longer history of rallying, which dates back to the 1907 Peking–Paris raid, and called upon all of this experience to join the battle. Both were driving each other on to raise their game, but they both recognised that the situation could not last for ever, and together with the FIA they established the tyre working group that laid out the

ABOVE Decisions, decisions… Eriksson tyre option in Argentina 1996.
(Prodrive)

BELOW Prodrive produced the gold-coloured magnesium Impreza wheels.
(Adam Warner)

proposals to limit the amount of testing and the number of tyres that could be used on a rally and defined where they could be changed. This working group is still in place today, as are the rules they helped to shape that kept the sport alive, particularly in the aftermath of the 2008 financial crash that played a key role in ending Subaru's long involvement with the sport.

Throughout the Impreza era their tyres were fitted to gold-coloured magnesium alloy Prodrive Speedline wheels, with bespoke sizes for asphalt, gravel and snow. These were:

- Tarmac: 18 x 8in SL856 (Type 2013)
- Gravel: 15 x 7in SL846 (Type 2011)
- Snow: 16 x 5.5in SL846 (Type 2011)

These magnesium rims were 1.5kg lighter per wheel than the steel options and gave an instant performance return, particularly in terms of acceleration and braking.

Specifications

Engine
- Flat-four 'boxer' quad-cam 16-valve
- Water injection
- Bore: 92mm
- Stroke: 75mm
- Capacity: 1,994cc
- Compression ratio: 8.8:1
- Power: Approx 330bhp @ 5,500rpm
- Power band: 2,500–6,000rpm
- Maximum engine speed: 8,000rpm
- Torque: Approx 340lb/ft @ 5,000rpm
- Air filter: Ramair

Transmission
- Prodrive six-speed semi-automatic pneumatic paddle shift plus H-pattern
- Front diff: active
- Centre diff: active
- Rear diff: locked
- Clutch: AP carbon

Turbo
- IHI VF15 RHB52 with 34mm restrictor as defined by FIA regulations
- Boost: 3 bar @ 2,500rpm

Control and display units
- Engine: FHI/STi
- Datalogging: GEMS
- Rally computer: Coralba
- Driver's instruments: Stack ST4000 0–8,000rpm tachometer
- VDO water temperature gauge

Exhaust
3in straight pipe with catalytic converter

Fuel system
75-litre boot-mounted safety tank

Suspension
- Bilstein MacPherson struts
- Springs   Asphalt: front 400–600lb, rear 250–450lb
           Gravel: front 160–275lb, rear 130–200lb

Wheels
- Speedline
- Asphalt: 18 x 8in
- Gravel: 15 x 7in
- Snow: 16 x 5.5in

Brakes
- AP callipers and vented discs
- Asphalt: front 366mm 6 pot, rear 304mm 4 pot
- Gravel: front 304mm 4 pot, rear 304mm 4 pot
- Snow: front 330mm 4 pot, rear 304mm 4 pot

Car dimensions
- Length: 4,340mm
- Width: 1,690mm
- Height: 1,405mm
- Wheelbase: 2,520mm
- Front track: 1,465mm
- Rear track: 1,465mm
- Weight: 1,230kg as defined by the FIA as the minimum weight

FIA homologation: A5480
- 1 April 1993–31 December 2010

Cockpit

(All pictures Adam Warner)

LEFT Always ensure there is no loose nut behind the wheel!

FAR LEFT The co-driver has control of the data logger and fire extinguisher.

LEFT There are no frills, but why would you need any?

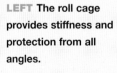

FAR LEFT Medical kit lives on the back seat in case of emergency.

LEFT The roll cage provides stiffness and protection from all angles.

FAR LEFT There are numerous fire-protection measures throughout the cabin.

LEFT The hanging pedals are mounted on a pedal box under the steering column.

RIGHT Simple and uncluttered dash display.

RIGHT Horn required for road legality, but seldom used.

FAR RIGHT Wiper controls are straight out of the road-going version.

RIGHT Keeping one eye on the engine temps is part of a rally driver's core skills.

FAR RIGHT Lights! Camera! Action! Vital for the night stages.

RIGHT Basic indicator control.

FAR RIGHT Brake-bias control.

LEFT Diff controls on the top left of instument panel.

LEFT Big red kill switch is often swapped for a heavier-duty version.

FAR LEFT The electronic data logger.

LEFT Driver-to-co-driver communication is vital.

Chapter Four

The driver's view

Tragically, three of the key drivers in the Group A Impreza story are no longer with us. But while we cannot hear the thoughts of Colin McRae, Richard Burns and 'Possum' Bourne, through Markku Alen, Ari Vatanen, Carlos Sainz and Pierro Liatti, we are given an amazing insight into what it was like to develop and compete in one of the most iconic rally cars of all time.

OPPOSITE Colin McRae celebrates his 1995 World Championship victory at the end of the RAC Rally, with Derek Ringer (left), Richard Burns (background) and Carlo Sainz (right). *(Sutton Motorsport Images)*

Not many drivers had the honour of driving a works Group A Subaru Impreza in the World Rally Championship. The first two to be granted this privilege were Finns Markku Alen and Ari Vatanen, who were behind the wheel of L555STE (Alen) and L555BAT (Vatanen).

Markku Alen

After 12 straight seasons with Lancia, during which time he'd racked up a then record 19 WRC wins, Alen joined Prodrive for the beginning of the Legacy project in 1990.

'At that time Prodrive was a very small team of about 40 mechanics in total,' he says. 'After so many years with Lancia it felt like year zero, but we were improving very quickly. All the time it was a big push but the biggest problem was budget. And the Legacy was not born to be a rally car. It was a little bit like a taxi – a beautiful taxi.'

After switching to Toyota for 1992, Alen returned to Subaru for 1993 and the Impreza's 1000 Lakes debut. Unfortunately he wouldn't make it to the end of the opening stage, but the development of the car was clear.

'I liked very much the handling,' he says. 'They were nice cars to drive. I liked the design of the Impreza, it was a beautiful rally car, and with the blue and gold colours it was a beautiful car. The Legacy was a great car to drive but it had no engine. It also had a beautiful noise – the boxer engine.'

Alen would never compete in another WRC round for Subaru, but he was welcomed back into the fold for a ten-day test in Kenya at the end of 1995 as part of the team's preparation for the following year's Safari Rally.

'I was in Kenya for two weeks with Colin McRae's co-driver Derek Ringer and the full team, and I felt that the car was improving a lot,' he remembers. 'We did simulating and testing at places like Caribou Lake, Nairobi – everywhere in Kenya. Colin had a big World Championship party and I was invited to do the test just before Christmas.'

All the suspension work that Alen carried out with the new Bilstein struts and remote oil reservoirs was rewarded by all three cars finishing in the top five.

Ari Vatanen

Ari Vatanen's relationship with Prodrive went back much further, as Prodrive founder David Richards was the Finn's co-driver when the pair won the 1981 World Championship in a Ford Escort. He joined Prodrive for the first time to campaign a Legacy in the 1991 RAC Rally and remained with the team for a limited programme for the following two seasons, culminating with the first two rallies for the new Impreza.

'We did some testing earlier in the summer in Finland and it felt good,' he says of his first outing in the Impreza. 'It was how the car made me feel – it was inspiring. It gave me confidence, and in order to really drive well the car must be confidence-inspiring. The Impreza was very much like a glove in my hands, a very nice, well-balanced car. It was nimbler than the Legacy.'

Vatanen backed up the highly encouraging second he scored on the 1000 Lakes with fifth place in what would be his final rally in the Group A Impreza – the 1993 RAC. With Carlos Sainz available for 1994 there was no place

TOP Vatanen was the 1981 World Champion for Ford. *(LAT)*

ABOVE Vatanen and Richards reunited with their Escort 1800T . *(LAT)*

LEFT Vatanen's second outing in the Impreza was in the 1993 RAC Rally. *(Prodrive)*

for Vatanen in the line-up, but he retains fond memories of the Impreza.

'I need a car that fits with my driving style and with the Subaru I was able to do it,' he says. 'I cannot stand an understeering car at all, and the Impreza did not understeer. I got it to my liking, and when the car is to your liking it gives you confidence and it's that confidence that makes the difference. It's all about your psychological mood. If you like a car and it inspires confidence, then as a driver you get wings.'

Carlos Sainz

As well as sponsorship from Repsol, Sainz brought with him a wealth of experience and a fine reputation as probably the best in the business at the time. He'd won two of the previous three championships, and following his stints with Toyota and Lancia had direct experience of the best cars that Group A had had to offer prior to the Impreza's introduction.

In fact, according to test team manager Ian Moreton it was Sainz's dedication and determination that accelerated the process of making the Impreza a world-beater. 'For me, the biggest single improvement we had on the car, bar none, was Carlos,' he states. 'Over everything else, that was the difference – he pushed engineering and particularly pushed David Lapworth to make it better. If you had a

problem when you were testing, David would say, "I'll get that sorted," and Carlos would press him for a timeframe. And if you said, "It'll be on Thursday," he would phone on Thursday and ask what was happening. He used to look around the car in great detail and would drive the test plan and would drive Pirelli very hard, whereas Colin would turn up and say, "Right, that's what we've got," and he'd test with it. And he'd give good feedback. But Carlos would press them about their development plan. He would phone Pirelli and ask if the tyres were on their way, and there were times when they'd have to send another little lorry with more tyres. That was the difference.'

The switch from Michelin to Pirelli tyres had taken place before the Spaniard was on board, but having won his two titles on the Italian rubber it was a move that he very much favoured. 'I was pleased because I knew the product very well and I had a really very good relationship with them all through my period with Toyota,' he recalls.

Sainz is credited with helping to get the Pirellis developed to suit the Impreza. As discussed earlier on, it was an era of extreme tyre development, and not just in terms of anti-puncture mousse systems. 'At that point, up to 1993, it was only Michelin who had mousse on the gravel tyre,' he says. 'But by the time of the Subaru we managed to have mousse tyres at Pirelli as well, and that was a very great help in all rallying, as you don't suffer any punctures when you use mousse.'

The elevated amount of testing helped Sainz and the team iron out the initial disparities between the Impreza's performances on gravel, which was always strong, and on asphalt, where it struggled to begin with.

'I felt immediately that the car had some potential,' he says. 'You could tell immediately that the car was different, because the boxer engine was unique in a Group A car. And although visually the car did not look very sporty, when you drove it you could feel it was very effective.'

Sainz's test-driving skills and feedback were also put to good use as Prodrive broke new ground in the WRC with the development of active diffs. Driver feedback was essential in corroborating the expected gains from the drawing board to actual performance on the stages.

BELOW Sainz was credited with being the driving force that turned the Impreza into a world beater. *(Prodrive)*

'Technically it was very advanced, and with Subaru and Prodrive we developed the first active diff in the car,' he says. 'Normally in a four-wheel-drive rally car the diffs are really important to the set-up. So when you have an active diff you can get the maximum help from the diff on braking to stabilise the car and not have too much locking.

'When you enter a corner and you open the diff you have some push and then you have some pivot, and then when the active diff detects some wheel-speed difference the pressure builds up. David Lapworth was the technical director and I have a lot of respect for him, and Christian Loriaux was his junior. I have good memories of the car and we developed it very quickly.'

ABOVE Sainz's first Subaru win came in the 1994 Acropolis Rally. *(Prodrive)*

LEFT The events of the 1995 Catalunya Rally soured the relationship between Sainz and McRae.

(Prodrive)

The development paid off with a maiden win on the 1994 Acropolis Rally, which was the foundation from which they could tilt at the championship. He missed out in the end on the final rally, the RAC, and history would repeat itself a year later.

Sainz rates his victory in the 1995 Monte Carlo Rally – the opening round of the season – as his finest in blue and gold. A further win in Portugal put him in the driving seat for the championship until a mountain bike accident left him with a broken shoulder and forced him to miss the New Zealand Rally.

He nevertheless had some reliability issues with the car, most notably in Sweden and Australia, which cost him points and also required him to act as an emergency mechanic.

'When you are testing, you always look at things a little bit, always ask, "What's this? How does it work?", that sort of thing,' he says. 'You train a little bit how to do some repairs, but I always depended on the car being reliable! I think you have to have certain bits of knowledge, but you always try to avoid problems. I was never very keen to be a super, super mechanic. I think you need to know a

little, but I prefer to work with the team before the rally to make the car reliable, rather than rely on my expertise as a mechanic!'

Sainz's fourth and final Impreza win came at home in the Rally Catalunya in circumstances neither he nor the team would have chosen. But the team orders that ultimately gave him the win only served to inspire Colin McRae even more, and it was the Scot who took the title with a scintillating drive in the RAC.

'Sometimes you can drive to the limit if you have confidence in a car. Sometimes you don't feel so confident, but with the Subaru I felt the confidence to push to the limit,' Sainz says. 'I had a strong teammate in Colin and this helped to drive me forward. It was a good period. Good memories.'

Pierro Liatti

Another key player in transforming the Impreza's performance on asphalt was Italian Pierro Liatti. Driving for the ART Engineering team, he was the first driver in Italy to run a Group A Impreza in 1994. At that year's San Remo event he was given full Prodrive

BELOW Sainz flies on his way to Rally Portugal victory in 1995. *(Prodrive)*

support, and he impressed the team sufficiently that he was brought into the works line-up for a part-time schedule in 1995.

With the full force of the factory behind him, Liatti benefitted from the latest updates, an effectively limitless supply of spares and a full test programme. On top of that he was paired with two of the greatest drivers of his generation: Sainz and McRae. 'It was a wonderful experience, I learned a lot from each of them,' he says. 'Colin was genius and recklessness when he was driving, Carlos was precision and meticulous attention to detail.

'Those years were very busy for me because I was the driver chosen to develop the car and also the tyres. Colin didn't love this part of the job so I was always going around the world testing. But it was interesting and rewarding, as we won the manufacturers' championship.'

Liatti did three WRC rounds for Prodrive in 1995, finishing eighth on his debut in Monte Carlo and sixth on the Tour de Corse, while in Corsica he recorded his first WRC podium in a Subaru 1-2-3, in a rally dominated by team orders that instructed McRae to hand the win to Sainz.

ABOVE McRae, Sainz and Liatti at Catalunya in 1995. *(Prodrive)*

BELOW Liatti on the 1995 Monte Carlo. *(Prodrive)*

'I was very happy for myself as it was my first result on a WRC event but I have to say that during the transfer from *parc fermé* to the press conference the atmosphere was very tense...' he recalls.

He did a full season in 1996, scoring three more podiums, which included second place finishes in Indonesia and Spain, but his finest hour came the following year at the start of the WRC era with victory in the 1997 Monte Carlo Rally.

LEFT Eriksson was second on the 1996 Safari Rally. *(Prodrive)*

Kenneth Eriksson

When Sainz left for Ford in 1996, Prodrive turned to Swede Kenneth Eriksson as his replacement. He'd made a strong impression during the '95 season, claiming two wins for Mitsubishi including a dominant win in Australia.

Second places in the Safari and Australia were the highlights of his season in the Group A car as he finished fourth in the championship and helped Subaru to defend its manufacturers' title.

He won on his debut in the WRC car in Sweden the following year and again in New Zealand mid-season, but after that his performances tailed off, and following the 1998 Swedish Rally he left the team.

Mats Jonsson and Didier Auriol

Another Swede, Mats Jonsson made a one-off appearance for the outfit in Sweden in 1995, and at the same venue a year later ex-World Champion Didier Auriol took his only start in a works Impreza. Jonsson retired, while Auriol battled with tyre issues to secure tenth place.

CENTRE Mats Jonsson on his sole Impreza WRC outing, on the 1995 Swedish Rally. *(LAT)*

RIGHT Auriol bagged a point on his only Impreza showing – Sweden again, in 1996. *(Prodrive)*

RIGHT McRae won more rallies in the Group A Impreza than anyone else. *(Prodrive)*

Absent heroes

Tragically, three of the select group who drove the Impreza Group A car are no longer with us. Colin McRae died in a terrible helicopter accident in 2007, in which three other people perished, including his five-year-old son Johnny. Richard Burns succumbed to a brain tumour aged just 34, and Peter 'Possum' Bourne was on his way to an event in New Zealand when he was involved in a head-on accident in which he suffered fatal head injuries.

McRae had been the poster boy for the Impreza, his total commitment and spectacular style winning him an army of fans the world over. He was by far the most successful driver in the car, taking seven of its 11 wins as well as the 1995 title.

Future World Champion Burns used an Impreza to score his maiden WRC podium on Rally GB 1995, while Bourne won the 1994 Asia Pacific Rally Championship behind the wheel of a works Group A Impreza.

BELOW Burns was a winner in the Asia-Pacific Championship in the Impreza. *(Prodrive)*

BELOW 'Possum' Bourne's relationship with Subaru pre-dated Prodrive's. *(Sutton Motorsport Images)*

ABOVE McRae on his way to a sensational win in the 1995 RAC Rally, and the world title. *(Prodrive)*

LEFT Burns flies on the 2001 Rally New Zealand. *(Prodrive)*

ABOVE Burns was the second of Subaru's three champions. *(Prodrive)*

RIGHT Bourne made just a handful of WRC appearences for the works team. *(LAT)*

Chapter Five

The co-driver's view

While it's the drivers who get the fame, adulation and the glory, none of their success would be possible without the note-reading, organisation and inspiration of their co-drivers. Unlike any other type of motorsport, rally driving is a team game and thanks to Robert Reid and Tony Sircombe, we are able to learn what life was like in the co-driver's seat of a Group A Impreza.

OPPOSITE Robert Reid partnered both Colin McRae and Richard Burns during their careers. *(Prodrive)*

the team tries to match the tyres and set-up to prevailing conditions.

Robert Reid

ABOVE Robert Reid co-drove for both Colin McRae and Richard Burns during his career. *(Prodrive)*

Robert Reid was Richard Burns' co-driver during his WRC career and before that in the British Rally Championship and the Asia Pacific series too. In the former the pair took over where Colin McRae and Derek Ringer left off, winning four rallies and the title for Prodrive in 1993. This success led to a call-up to the WRC programme for Rally GB in the Legacy's final outing for the factory team. They finished seventh which led directly to a maiden outing in the Impreza, as Reid recalls.

'Our transition into the Group A Impreza was through the Group A Legacy. We won the British National Championship in 1992, and the British Open Championship with a Group A Legacy in 1993. And then from Rally GB '93 we flew almost directly to Thailand to do the last round of the Asia Pacific, and that was the first time that we drove the Group A Impreza.'

For 1994 and 1995 Burns and Reid were part of Subaru's assault on the Asia Pacific championship, which also incorporated WRC rounds in New Zealand and Australia. This was a golden era in the championship's history. It started in 1988, but by the mid-1990s the Japanese manufacturers were taking it very seriously, and with the Far East being a key market for Prodrive's title sponsor 555 the Asia Pacific set-up was almost at the scale of the full WRC armada.

In 1993 Kiwi Peter 'Possum' Bourne had taken the Asia Pacific title in the Legacy, and while that car may have lacked the outright pace to be a true contender at WRC level, its robustness was a great asset in the less developed stages of the APRC.

'The Legacy was one of those cars, and I've heard people say it about the Manta 400 as well, that was almost like a limousine,' says Reid. 'It was really spacious and quite big. And then all of a sudden the Impreza was quite small, but apart from that it was pretty familiar.'

It was a period of rapid development in top-

Unlike most other forms of motorsport, rallying is a two-person effort, and while it's the driver who tends to get the lion's share of the glory, ultimately they all acknowledge that without a world-class co-driver alongside them their success would not have been possible.

There's much more to the co-driver role than simply calling the pace notes. In fact, to varying degrees they have to be administrators and mechanics as well as a sounding board as

LEFT Reid and Burns celebrate winning Rally New Zealand in 2001. *(LAT)*

flight rallying and Reid would play a key role in helping the process of refining the technology and determining how to get the most out of it in a competitive environment.

'Different drivers have different views on testing,' says Reid. 'Richard's view was always that there were only ever two of us in the car in competition, so therefore anything I could glean from testing was useful for him in competition. If he took an engineer in the car for a test, that was fine for the test but it wasn't really going to wash for the actual competition. And he always wanted me to read notes on the test, his view being that if I was reading notes he was driving automatically. He therefore had the spare capacity to feel and think about what was happening with the car.'

Co-drivers are contracted to the teams rather than individual drivers and as such tend to move around the service parks, especially when new drivers enter the fray or more established ones are struggling for form. It's a small community, but even so Reid is unique in having partnered Colin McRae, his younger brother Alister and Burns in three successive events.

'I did the Hackle Rally – a Scottish Championship round – with Colin in 1990, in his uncle Huw's Mk2 Escort with a Pinto engine in – and we won. I then did the Galloway Hills with Alister in December, and then the Wyedean with Richard in the Peugeot 309 at the end of January. Within a five-month period I'd driven with all three of them.'

Reid co-drove with McRae again during a test session in the Impreza in New Zealand in 1994, so had first-hand experience of how Britain's two WRC title winners handled the Impreza.

'I remember on that test with Colin going to various different roads, and going back again with Richard a number of days later,' he says, 'and speaking to Lappy [David Lapworth] at the time, Colin set the fastest time of that day on the second or third run up that road. Richard set the fastest time of the day on his tenth run up the road, but it was a couple of tenths faster than McRae went.

'And I think as a driver that's where you develop. You've got the speed, then it's

having the confidence in the notes. And one thing about the Impreza was that it was a confidence-inspiring car. Although Richard's driving style was not necessarily the same as Colin's it wasn't that far off it. It didn't matter if the car was sideways coming into the corner as long as the wheels – steering wheel included – were facing the right way at the apex and you had maximum drive out of the corner.'

Of course that technique doesn't always

BELOW **Reid checks his pacenotes as Burns readies himself for action.** *(LAT)*

ABOVE **Burns and Reid on their way to victory in the Australian Rally in 1999.** (LAT)

But sometimes the damage is repairable, and on these occasions the co-driver has to get stuck in, although their mechanical competence and knowledge can vary dramatically. 'Because Richard had built all his own rally cars, he knew what he was doing. He had a lighter touch than I did being a farmer boy and being used to big socket sets and big nuts and bolts, so it would tend to be "Hand me this, hand me that, turn this, turn that." Richard was never too happy with me doing the wheel nuts up with the torque wrench, because being a farmer I was used to doing nuts up until they creaked three times for them to be tight enough, which in the days of precision engineering wasn't exactly what was needed!'

Tony Sircombe

In contrast, their counterparts in the Asia Pacific line-up, 'Possum' Bourne and his co-driver Tony Sircombe, came from a slightly older, more hands-on generation.

'Possum and I both grew up in the early days of rallying in New Zealand in the early 1980s. The cars were a lot simpler – we're talking Mk2 Escorts – and everyone built their own cars,' he says. 'I was involved with my old teams after hours from my real job – I was in the Air Force at the time. So at night I'd be preparing and building rally cars for the season.

work. McRae had a couple of periods in his career where he suffered sizeable accidents in consecutive events, and while Burns was never regarded as a crasher per se, there were a few occasions where the Impreza was brought back looking decidedly second-hand.

'We had a rather dramatic accident that involved a large piece of New Zealand and when we came to a rest the floor was ripped,' Reid says. 'And we looked up and there was DR [David Richards] and Ryuichiro Kuze standing watching, having landed the helicopter. So that wasn't a particularly high point!'

RIGHT **'Possum' Bourne struggled with the smaller air restrictor on the 1995 Rally Australia.** (Prodrive)

So you had to be hands-on and that meant you understood it, but that said it was also very simple technology. Possum was very much the same right from when he started rallying. He had his own workshop where he would build his own cars. Right up until pretty much the Prodrive days he built the cars himself.

'Possum was a very competent mechanic. I think because he had grown up with Subaru from the mid-'80s, when he started with them, and the Safari work that he did, he was very competent in his understanding and his ability to get the car home. So to a certain extent I followed his lead, as the Subaru was new to me. Between us we were pretty hands-on, so we could figure out what was going on.'

Bourne's involvement with Subaru comfortably pre-dated Prodrive's, going back to the Safari programme that started in 1986 with the Group A Leone. He also achieved the marque's first top-three finish with third place on the Rally New Zealand in 1987.

Tragically his co-driver Rodger Freeth succumbed to injuries he sustained in a crash on the 1993 Rally Australia. Sircombe had most recently been working with Rod Millen as part of Mazda's WRC programme, but since that had been cancelled at the end of 1992 he was available. He'd worked with Prodrive before, as co-driver for American Jon Woodner in the BMW M3 in 1987 in the European Rally Championship.

Together they wrapped up back-to-back Asia Pacific titles in 1993 and 1994, firstly in a Legacy and then in the Impreza. That version, with the 38mm air restrictor, was Sircombe's favourite.

'In '94 the car was an incredible jump forward from the Legacy,' he says. 'For a start you had this small, very nimble car, but the big difference even to '95 was the fact that it still had the larger 38mm restrictor. So it was a really powerful car. And you could really move it around – it was very active. It was very noticeable in '95 when they choked it down to 34mm, which made the car a completely different animal to drive. The best days with the Impreza were in '94. It had 380bhp or something and for sure it was an exciting time to drive.'

The pair's success in the Asia Pacific was

never carried over to their occasional WRC entries, with seventh on the 1995 Rally New Zealand the best they managed in four World Championship outings. In contrast there were three APRC wins and an against-the-odds fourth place in the 1995 Hong Kong–Beijing Rally.

When the pair arrived on the Chinese mainland in 1995 for the first proper leg it became clear to Bourne that something was amiss with the car. Faced with a 4,000km drive through China they initially took it easy before diagnosing some pretty severe engine issues. Using their skills and intuition they somehow managed to nurse the car along, dragging it smoking and wheezing to the ceremonial finish in Tiananmen Square, where the flywheel promptly fell off, meaning that they couldn't turn the engine off as it would never restart.

Although Bourne would remain with Subaru for the rest of his career, he wouldn't be a part of Prodrive's official works line-up again after 1995. Sircombe remained with the brand too, mentoring Subaru junior driver Shigeyuki Konishi in 1997. After a brief stint with Mitsubishi working with Hamed Al-Wahaibi, he teamed up with Japan's most successful rally driver Toshihiro Arai, running in series across the world in a succession of Imprezas from 2002 to 2007. These days Sircombe is offering career guidance to rising Indonesian racer Sean Galael, who started off in rallying (with Sircombe co-driving) before switching to track racing.

ABOVE Sircombe continued his relationship with Subaru and Toshihiro Arai. *(Sutton Motorsport Images)*

Chapter Six

Running a Group A Impreza today

Only a small handful of the 63 Group A Imprezas that Prodrive built are in active service today, but many of those other museum pieces have been restored and kept in a condition where they could be readied to compete at short notice. Because the car was fundamentally quite simple, there is a limit to what can go wrong, but as we discover in this chapter keeping 20-plus-year-old technology in action can be a tricky and arduous process.

OPPOSITE The fans love seeing the Group A Impreza in action at historic events. N555 BAT is seen here on the forest rally stage at the 2017 Goodwood Festival of Speed. *(Tom Rendle)*

133

ABOVE Ryan
Champion owns and
runs the Group A
Impreza driven by
Liatti during 1996.
(Prodrive)

In total, Prodrive built 63 Subaru Imprezas to Group A spec. Only nine of these were used in the World Rally Championship. The rest were either run by Prodrive in the Asia Pacific Rally Championship, or as part of the All Stars team in 1997, or were sold to private individuals.

Cars ended up all over the world – the US, Japan and quite a lot in Europe, where they were a formidable proposition in series like the Irish Tarmac Rally Championship and its equivalents in France, Belgium and Italy. In fact, the final two cars to leave Prodrive went to Bertie Fisher in Ireland and the last of all to Belgium.

Because so many cars were built, and spread so widely, knowledge of how to keep the cars up and running has travelled with them, although initially all servicing took place back in Prodrive's base in Banbury.

Of the 63 Group A Imprezas that were registered (a number of Group N versions have been 'up-specced' over the years), it is estimated that fewer than ten are still in regular competitive use, although quite a few more are kept in running order for appearances at historic events such as the Goodwood Festival of Speed and Race Retro. One of these cars

is owned by Ryan Champion, who has N555 BAT, the car that was driven by Didier Auriol on his one-off rally for Subaru in Sweden in 1996, before being campaigned by Piero Liatti for the majority of the rest of the season.

Champion, who's been competing on the stages around the world since 1992, uses the expertise of BGMsport, which has become one of the foremost specialists in the restoration and preparation of Group A Imprezas. In fact, Ian Gwynne at BGM reckons at some point every one of the original 63 cars has passed through its workshop in Brackley.

Because pretty much every part bar the body panels on the Impreza is bespoke, keeping the car original is not easy, but there is sufficient expertise available to find a solution to pretty much every problem.

One of the areas that causes the biggest headaches is the transmission. The active front and centre diffs mean that there is a maze of hydraulic piping surrounding the gearbox and it's essential that these are maintained correctly to keep it running properly.

Although the internals were originally designed by Prodrive, which in turn supplied the spares to customers in period, BGM has subsequently designed and built its own replacement parts so that owners can service their cars without the need for a works-backed WRC budget. Although they were unable to make exact copies of the original Prodrive parts, by making subtle alterations – adjusting the tooth angle by a degree or two – they were able to create low-cost alternatives that are unnoticeably different from the original from the driving seat. 'The good thing from our point of view is that we know a lot of people who used to be there in period who can help out with bits and information,' says Gwynne.

For the past few years it was the Group B cars that got rally car collectors' juices flowing, but with those cars having found their homes attention has now turned to the Group A machines, of which the Impreza is one of the most famous and desirable. As a result, the demand for restoration has been on the rise.

The process of restoration raises the usual key question: should the car be restored back to the specification it was in period, or should it be prepared to a condition in which it can be used in anger on a rally today?

Restoring the cars to their true original spec is no mean feat. They are now over 20 years old and a lot has changed in that time, particularly in the world of engine management. Restoring the car so that it features the original GEMS data logger, for example, can open a real can of worms. 'I think the map writing is done in DOS,' suggests Gwynne, 'and I think the data logger is Windows 95.' This, combined with the fact that all the information has to be burnt on to EPROM chips, means that the temptation is to fit a modern ECU. Although it may not always be quite as simple as that.

'We tried the sensible route of putting it on a modern management system, which should have meant it was easy to map and easy to run,' says Champion. 'But it didn't work, for no logical reason.'

'There is no logical reason,' Gwynne similarly asserts. 'Basically the board that was used was from a Group N car. Fundamentally all the controls in the ECU are the same. We put one of the ECUs Ryan had on his car on one of my cars and it had the same problem it had on Ryan's car. There was some sort of bug in it. I reckon it

was something to do with it going through the logger, whereas in a Group N car it was straight. There's something in the software that didn't like running through the chassis looms of the car and through the loggers, and I'm convinced it's something to do with the logger.'

The data logger and the ECU aren't the only parts of the Impreza that are difficult to restore to original specification. On the cars that left the Prodrive work bays the wheels were fitted by means of titanium studs. While these are a nice, lightweight and well-engineered part, they were built for use by a full WRC team and its army of professional mechanics. There was no issue if

ABOVE Most private owners have replaced the titanium wheel studs with steel ones.
(Adam Warner)

LEFT Over- or under-tightning the nuts can lead to the studs shearing.
(Adam Warner)

RIGHT **Internal kill switch was a bit lightweight and easily breakable on original car.** *(Adam Warner)*

BELOW **External kill switch is easy to locate.** *(Adam Warner)*

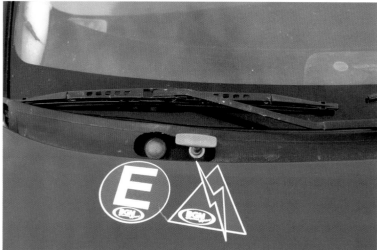

the wheel nuts were correctly tightened, but if the nuts weren't torqued correctly or left loose the stress this created on the studs could cause them to snap. So since the mid-1990s people such as BGM have been offering a replacement service where steel wheel studs were added when the hubs were rebuilt. Such was the commonness of this problem that pretty much all of the Group A Imprezas now have steel studs. They might be heavier, but they are a much more reliable solution.

One of the Impreza's key strengths in period was its reliability, and despite its age this still holds true today if the car is regularly maintained. However, age has taken its toll on a lot of the sensors, particularly on the gearbox, and these parts – which originally came off a JCB – are no longer available. As a result replacement sensors were created, and with the help of GEMS a new gearbox map was created.

Many people have also replaced the kill switch – which was a bit lightweight and fragile – with a more robust version, while a lot of Group A Imprezas have a single ventilation scope (taken from the WRC version) on the

LEFT **Many owners have replaced the twin air vents with the WRC's more effective single vent.** *(Adam Warner)*

LEFT Universal joint on gear linkage is another common failure. *(Adam Warner)*

roof, rather than the twin design that was present in period, and was far less effective at keeping the cabin cool and well aired.

Another common fault is the failure of the universal joint at the end of the gearlever, where it meets with the selector housing, which is prone to breaking. A simple fix is to install the UJ from the steering column. The piece works in exactly the same way but is much more robust and effectively unbreakable. Of course, it's heavier, but the few extra grams of mass is unlikely to make a discernable difference to overall performance. However, anyone seeking to restore the car to its exact original specification will still want to use the original part. A lot of people have added carbon door inner skins, but these were not standard on the Group A Impreza, which took the window winder and plastic fittings directly out of the road car.

There should be a black central piece behind where the door handle is located, while the overall skin is a very dark grey. At the rear the lining also same out of a standard road car, again with wind-up windows. Remarkably these had a normal fabric insert as opposed to vinyl and are almost impossible to source replacement parts for.

But by far the biggest problem with creating a car to totally original spec is the turbocharger. The original IHI turbo – the VF15

BHB52 – is no longer in production and is virtually impossible to source. As Champion says, if you have an original 'you wrap it in cotton wool or put it on a shelf in a box'. On his own car he's replaced the turbo with a similar unit from a road-going WRX. There's a small penalty to pay in terms of power and torque – especially torque at the top of the rev range – but with the original turbos changing hands for upwards of £8,000 it's a sensible and practical solution.

The availability of numerous reproductions of the driveshafts, CV joints and suspension components means that sourcing spares

BELOW The original cars had a simple black piece of plastic as door lining. *(Adam Warner)*

ABOVE The extreme conditions the cars experience in rallies means that damage is inevitable. *(Prodrive)*

BELOW Most owners want their cars to be as close to the original spec as possible. *(Prodrive)*

for these parts is easy, although according to Gwynne 'the outer driveshaft bits are a bit awkward'.

Perhaps the most famous restoration BGM completed was that of L555BAT, which was the car that was given to Colin McRae and is now in the possession of his father Jimmy. McRae senior drove the Legacy BGM had prepared for the Goodwood FoS and was so impressed by the experience that he sent the Impreza down to be worked on.

The car had been sitting idle for years. Water had been left in the engine, which had caused it to corrode, as had the fuel lines and all the brake lines. As the car had sat for so long, the fluid had solidified in the brake lines, and all the grease had gone hard in the hubs and diffs, and the seals had gone too. Consequently the engine was completely stripped down, but remarkably the original turbo was still salvageable. After around three months the rebuild was complete, and the car was sent back up to the McRae home in Scotland.

Once an Impreza WRX has been prepared, getting it ready for action is a relatively straightforward process. A complete fluid

change – gearbox, differential and engine oil, brake fluids and coolants – is required. These are off-the-shelf products and readily available from specialist retailers. The fuel, oil and air filters are also replaced. These were originally Prodrive-built components, with a blue-painted oil filter weighing in at £130! Again, off-the-shelf replacement parts for these are easy to find.

After the fluids and filters have been changed, the next step is to do a full check of all the joints in the suspension and transmission to see if there are any cracks, and if the answer is no the car is effectively good to go.

If the car is still using the original ECU and engine mapping, then it will only run on special race fuel. In period this was Elf turbo plus, but of course any 102RON-spec fuel will suffice, although at £4 a litre it's not cheap, and with the super-thin Aeroquip fuel lines any fuel left in the system will quickly evaporate if the car is left standing.

As a matter of course the engine is cranked over by hand before the fuel is added just to get the oil to circulate, and then it's ready to be fired up … or not! 'They either start, or they don't start! There's no in between,' says Champion.

In order to get the car going the first step is to ensure that the battery has the correct voltage in it. To avoid any doubt, a lot of people employ an auxiliary battery just to get it started and into its warm-up mode.

When the car doesn't start, invariably the spark plugs have been flooded and there's no option but to get them out, which is not the work of a moment. The front chassis leg restricts access to the front two plugs, and if the car isn't perhaps as straight as it should be could make this process very tricky. Also, the coil pack is tricky to remove and re-attach due to its positioning.

It's best practice with the car to remove all the pressure from the hydraulic system on the gearbox after use. This is achieved by standing on the footbrake, pulling on the handbrake and then popping out the circuit breaker. This takes all the pressure out of the system and protects the seal, which at £600 each is worth treating with care.

Most of the Imprezas that are in active service have changed the dampers. The original fixed-rate Bilsteins worked well in period, but damper design has come a long way over the past 20

years. 'On the old dampers, the hotter they got and the longer the stage the worse they got,' says Gwynne, 'whereas the modern dampers have just got better valving, better oil and better control, so remain more stable from the start of the stage to the end rather than tailing off.'

So for a privateer running a car on a limited budget, fitting adjustable dampers makes a lot of sense. However, the art of tuning the dampers to improve the balance of the car can often confuse and frustrate the inexperienced and the unprepared. Making unnecessary or incorrect changes can make the car almost undrivable, so care needs to be taken when adjusting the rebound rates to ensure that they are adjusted in the same way all the way around.

Of course, there's no issue in finding tyres, with a wide array of options available. But as Champion says: 'I feel a sense of obligation to run it on Pirellis because that's what it was always on.'

Because so many Group N cars have been converted to resemble Group A cars, to the unwary it's easy to be fooled into thinking a car is something that it isn't. However, there are a number of key signs that are obvious giveaways that a car isn't a Prodrive original.

Scott McBurney owns a pair of Group A Imprezas – a 1996 car that went on to be a part of the All Stars programme in 1997 and a 1995 version ex-McRae car that was bought by long-

ABOVE Modern adjustable dampers are more user-friendly than the original versions.
(Adam Warner)

ABOVE Details on the weld can distinguish original Prodrive cars.
(Adam Warner)

OPPOSITE The Impreza is normally a reliable runner if looked after properly.
(Steve Rendle)

time Prodrive backer Freddy Dor. As a result, he's become well-versed in knowing exactly what to look out for…

'Quite a lot of cars have been re-shelled to look like a Prodrive car, but if you've seen a Prodrive car they are pretty easy to spot,' he reckons. 'The obvious giveaway is the roll cage: you've got the butterfly welding on the door pillar on each side behind the driver's head, and there's a specific curve in it that's hard to replicate. There are various brackets to hold the wiring loom in place in the tunnel and underneath the dash, and then in the boot the brackets that hold in the spare wheel carrier – where they are mounted for the strap one should always be above where the exhaust pipe

is at the rear, and the other is the spare turbo mount, behind the driver's seat.'

While restoring his '96-spec car, McBurney, who brought it over from France, discovered something that can be an issue with some Imprezas – chassis rot. Prodrive routinely dipped the shells in an acid bath to remove the paint. However, the cars were not neutralised afterwards. This wasn't a problem for the works cars that would be regularly redipped and repainted, but for cars that went off into private hands this left a legacy that could cause issues further down the line.

When McBurney stripped down his car he found that some problems with the floor had been masked by simply welding new pieces over the rot, effectively sandwiching the corroded floor and making it invisible.

'It had eaten away at itself all the way out to the inner sills,' he says. 'The tinworm went right through it. So all that had to be cut out and replaced, and that was a bit of a surprise. I was worried that we would lose the cage, but it was all alright. It was just the floor pan and the inner sills.'

For cars that have led a competitive life on the gravel stages – where dints, dents and damage are inevitable – chassis rot is a common problem. E-coating is the best way of preventing this.

All in all, if it's looked after regularly and properly an Impreza WRX ought to be a reliable, relatively easy – if not inexpensive – car to own and run.

RIGHT The mounting points for the spare wheel are another tell-tale sign.
(Adam Warner)

The rivals

Subaru joined the rally fraternity at a time when some of the most successful manufacturers in the sport's history were active. While the WRC rules would allow a host of new names to enter the fray, when the Impreza hit the stages it went head-to-head against the best that Ford, Lancia and Toyota had to offer, while another newcomer that would establish a rich rallying history was also gearing up for greatness: Mitsubishi.

Ford Escort RS Cosworth

Thanks to models such as the Mark I RS1600 and Mexico and the Mark II RS1800, Ford's Escort was the most prolific car in rallying history. However, the planned Group B-spec Mark III RS1700T was canned before it ever competed, although the Blue Oval did return to the stages with the RS200.

BELOW Delecour in his traditional all-out attack style in 1993. *(LAT)*

There were no motorsport variants of the Mark IV, but with the fifth generation, introduced in 1990, came the RS Cosworth, a super-hot hatch designed to replace the legendary Sierra Cosworth that had enjoyed considerable motorsport success on track as well as in rallying.

Introduced in 1992, in reality the RS Cosworth was little more than a re-bodied Sierra and not really an Escort at all, but nevertheless, plans were soon under way for a rallying programme, which kicked off in the Spanish Championship in 1992 with Jose Maria Bardolet, while Ford mainstay Malcolm Wilson gave it a British debut in the Scottish Rally, although he was not formally registered for the event.

Towards the end of 1992 Ford Motorsport officially stopped development of the Sierra Cosworth and all attention was switched to the Escort, which would be its sole focus for the 1993 season. In order to get the necessary homologation Ford built 2,500 of the Motorsport version of the RS Cosworth road car. Fitted with a massive Garrett T3/T04B turbo from the RS200, these were stripped-out versions that had the sunroof and some sound-deadening removed, and were genuinely more suited to the stages than the road.

A works Ford Escort returned to the stages for the first time since 1981 for the opening round of the 1993 championship, the Monte Carlo Rally. It was very nearly a winning debut too, as François Delecour went head-to-head with the Toyota Celica of Didier Auriol, missing out by just 15 seconds by the finish. With Miki Biasion finishing third, it was an encouraging start for the new programme.

The works cars skipped the next round in Sweden but made a winning return in Portugal, where Delecour led home Biasion for an Escort 1-2. There were four more wins that season, with Delecour prevailing on the Tour de Corse and again in Catalunya, Biasion ending a three-year winless streak on the Acropolis, and

tarmac ace Franco Cunico scoring the only WRC win of his career in a version privately entered by Ford Italia on the San Remo.

When Delecour won the opening round of 1994 a title charge seemed to be on its way, but it was a false dawn, as a month later he was severely injured in a road accident when his Ferrari F40 was struck by an amateur rally driver, leaving Delecour with serious leg injuries that kept him out of the next four rallies; he would never win a WRC event again. Tommi Makinen scored the first of his 24 WRC wins with an Escort Cosworth later in the year, but it was an ultimately disappointing return and at the end of the year Ford passed responsibility for the development of the car to RAS Sport, which had just clinched the European Rally Championship with an RS Cosworth driven by Patrick Snijers.

The turbo restriction reduction for 1995 hurt Ford more than most – their 1995 season was a disaster and not a single win, or indeed top-three finish, was recorded. This prompted Ford to take the development back in-house for 1996, and in the hands of new signing Carlos Sainz victory was secured on the inaugural Rally Indonesia, and four further top-three finishes took him to third place in the drivers' championship.

The switch to WRC rules in 1997 gave Ford – and Wilson's M-Sport team entrusted with developing the cars – a chance to overcome some of the Escort's inherent shortcomings. Among these were the engine's sluggish performance at the lower end of the rev range, a consequence of the oversized turbo it had employed in the quest for ultimate power at the start of the programme, and the enormous amount of turbo lag it created. However, the Ford was one of the most potent engines of the era, probably producing upwards of 370bhp with the 38mm restrictor.

The 1993 Cosworth YBT engine was longitudinally mounted, which wasn't the ideal layout for optimising weight distribution. In rally form it was heavily modified, with the crankshaft made from a single piece of steel, titanium driveshafts and forged aluminium pistons. The outlet valves had lithium inlays, while the valves in general were wider than the road car version.

The drivers could operate a 'bang, bang' firing order from the cockpit. This was a system developed in motorcycle racing, where the ignition order is arranged so that the power strokes occur simultaneously, ie rather than, say, 1, 3, 2, 4 it goes 12, 34. This is an attempt to balance power delivery and is a crude form of traction control.

The RS Cosworth was fitted with a seven-speed gearbox mated to a dual-plate carbon clutch. Like the Impreza it had active front and centre diffs and a mechanical rear diff. Another change was in the rear suspension. The semi-trailing arm used in the Group A car gave it a skittish, understeery handling characteristic, and it was replaced by the more conventional MacPherson strut layout used in the Impreza.

ABOVE Sainz took his first win in an Escort on the inaugural Rally Indonesia in 1996. *(LAT)*

Lancia Delta HF Integrale Evo

By the time the Impreza appeared on the scene the Delta was of almost pensionable age and very clearly past its best, but this was the car to beat during the formative years of the Group A era.

Lancia had a formidable rally pedigree that dated back to the Fulvia in the 1960s and carried on through the Stratos, 037 and the Group B Delta S4. When the latter became obsolete after the Group B cars were outlawed, Lancia set to work on developing the Group A version of its five-door hatchback, which had been introduced to the road car market way back in 1979.

Designed by Giorgetto Giugiario's Italdesign company, the front-wheel-drive hatch was voted the European Car of the Year in 1980 and was initially available with uninspiring 1,300cc and 1,500cc engine options. Following a facelift in 1982 the first of the HF 'High Fidelity' hot hatch models was introduced in 1983 and featured a turbocharged 1.6-litre engine. A special edition HF Martini version followed in 1984 with Martini racing stickers and was a prelude to what was to follow in 1987.

The S4 version that was required for Group B homologation was unveiled in October 1985. Priced at 100 million Italian *lire*, these were the most expensive Lancias of all time, but the 200 units that were built are now genuine collectors' items and worth way more than the purchase price at the time!

Alongside the S4, Lancia introduced an updated version of the HF, the HF turbo. Following yet another facelift in 1986 this was updated again into the HF 4WD, which had a new, bigger 2-litre engine as well as four-wheel drive, and was the car that formed the basis for the Group A car of 1987.

Lancia hit the ground running in 1987, and although the car was compromised by its small wheels – and therefore brakes – and limited suspension travel, it was more than a match for the Mazda 323, Ford Sierra RS Cosworth and BMW M3, and between them works drivers Miki Biasion, Markku Alen and Juha Kankkunen and privateer Franz Wittmann – who won for the brilliantly named Funkberaterring Rally Team in the absence of the works cars on Rally New Zealand – won nine of the championship's 13 rounds. Kankkunen was the drivers' champion and Lancia scored almost double the points of Audi as it ran away with the manufacturers' crown.

The HF 4WD was deployed to victory in the opening two rounds of 1988 before it was replaced by the HF Integrale. Featuring bigger wheels, larger brakes, beefed-up suspension and more power, the Integrale picked up where the 4WD left off and took eight more wins courtesy of Biasion, Alen and Jorge Recalde, who scored his only WRC win on that year's Rally Argentina. Biasion claimed his first drivers' championship, while Lancia was even more dominant in the manufacturers' contest, outscoring Ford by 140 to 79.

Fitted with a new, stronger six-speed gearbox the HF Integrale carried on into 1989 and Biasion and new teammate Didier Auriol reeled off five straight wins to get the title defence off to a flying start. But Toyota had introduced its Celica GT-4 – the most credible challenger to the Delta's dominance so far – and it showed its potential with a 1-2 trouncing of the Lancias at the 1000 Lakes.

Lancia hit back with the introduction of the HF Integrale 16v, which as the name suggests featured a 16-valve version of the 1,995cc inline four-cylinder double overhead camshaft, transversely-mounted engine. With a boost in horsepower, Lancia was ready to take on the challengers, and victory on its debut in the San Remo was enough for Biasion to secure back-to-back drivers' championships and for Lancia to secure a hat-trick of manufacturers' titles.

The HF Integrale 16v continued into 1990 and claimed six rally wins for Auriol, Biasion and Kankkunen, who had returned to the team after a couple of seasons with Toyota. However, as the wins were shared around this opened the door for Toyota's Carlos Sainz to mount a championship charge. Victory in the season showdown – the RAC Rally – was the Spaniard's fourth of the season, and, with Kankkunen crashing out, it earned him the championship. This meant that for the first time in Group A history someone other than a Lancia driver was the champion. But the Delta still cleaned up in the manufacturers' standings, though a winning margin of just six points over Toyota suggested that its era of dominance was coming to an end.

However, that was underestimating the Delta's trump card – its near bullet-proof reliability. Honed and refined over five tough years of competition and underscored by an almost endless budget, not to mention having drivers of the calibre of Kankkunen and Auriol on its books, Lancia fought back in 1991. And when Sainz's Celica blew a head gasket on the RAC Rally, Kankkunen reclaimed the drivers' title for the Italian marque, while it yet again cleaned up in the manufacturers' stakes.

There was no getting away from the fact that the Delta was getting old, but Lancia had one final trick up its sleeve and that was the HF Integrale Evo, which was introduced ahead of the 1992 season. With outrageously wide wheel arches it represented one last stab at curing the Delta's Achilles' heel – its underpowered brakes and limited suspension travel. It also had completely revised aero, a significantly more powerful engine and a new, stiffer body.

But the Evo would not be run by the factory team, which officially withdrew at the end of 1991. Instead, the ultimate Group A Delta would be run by the independent Jolly Club team, although given that financing was coming from the factory this was stretching the definition of independent to its limits.

Revelling in the new Delta's performance, Auriol set a new record for wins in a single season with six, while the consistent Kankkunen remained in the title fight with victory in Portugal. However, when Auriol's engine blew and Kankkunen made a mistake on the RAC title-decider, it allowed Sainz to slip through and claim the championship against the odds.

Italian Andrea Aghini scored his first and only WRC win in San Remo that year, and would go into the record books as the last driver to win a World Rally Championship event for Lancia.

BELOW There would be no wins for Lancia or Sainz in 1993. The ex-Sainz car is seen here at the Goodwood Festival of Speed in 2007. *(LAT)*

Although it claimed a record sixth straight manufacturers' title in 1992, it was clear that its best days were behind it.

Auriol and Kankkunen moved to Toyota for 1993 while World Champion Sainz moved the other way and brought his Repsol sponsorship with him. However, the assurances he had that Lancia would continue to back the programme turned out to be false. He managed second place on the Acropolis Rally, a result he repeated in San Remo before he was disqualified for fuel irregularities.

When Jolly Club opted to skip the RAC Rally, the Delta's Group A adventure was brought to a close. In total there were 46 wins and four drivers' titles, while the record of six straight manufacturers' championships still stands to this day.

Mitsubishi Lancer Evo I/II/III

Unlike Ford, Lancia and Toyota, Mitsubishi had no real rallying pedigree before the creation of the Group A era. Its Ralliart performance arm was established by Andrew Cowan and Doug Stewart in 1983, and the Rugby-based team was entrusted with developing its first official full-time WRC challenger, the Galant VR-4.

The Galant shared some underpinnings with an aborted Starion Group B project, and it was homologated in time for the 1988 season. It made its debut on the 1988 Rally New Zealand

with Kenjiro Shinozuka. The Japanese driver would go on to win that season's inaugural Asia Pacific Rally Championship for Mitsubishi – its most high-profile success to date.

The Galant's only other official outing that year came when Ralliart entered two cars in the RAC Rally, one for Shinozuka and another for 1981 World Champion Ari Vatanen, who was rebuilding his career after his life-threatening accident in the 1985 Rally Argentina. Vatanen retired with engine problems and Shinozuka was a very distant 26th.

The car was much improved for the 1989 season, good enough for Michael Ericsson to score Mitsubishi's first WRC win in the 1000 Lakes, while at the end of the season popular Finn Pentti Airikkala recorded his only WRC win when he triumphed in the RAC Rally.

In the absence of any of the works teams, Frenchman Patrick Tauziac won the Ivory Coast Rally in the VR-4 in 1990, a feat repeated by Shinozuka in 1991 and 1992. The Galant's only other WRC success came in 1991, when Kenneth Eriksson came out on top in his home event in Sweden.

Much as Subaru had surmised with the Legacy, Mitsubishi came to the conclusion that the Galant was simply too big for the demands of modern rallying, and for 1993 Ralliart started to develop a competition version of its mid-sized

saloon, the Lancer. The first Mitsubishi to bear the Lancer name was released in 1973, and a beefed-up version of the 1600GSR had been driven to victory on the East African Safari Rally by Joginder Singh in 1974 and again in 1976.

The Lancer, badged as a Colt in some markets and known as a Mirage in others, had been through a number of iterations by the time the next generation was launched in October 1991. These were pretty humdrum mass-market family cars, but a year later a version was released that would come to redefine the brand. This was the Lancer Evolution I. Featuring a 2-litre, DOHC engine and a four-wheel-drive system taken directly from the Galant VR-4, this was a stripped-down street racer with almost the ideal proportions for a Group A rally car.

The Lancer made its full WRC debut in the 1993 Monte Carlo Rally, where a pair of Ralliart-built cars was entered for Eriksson and German Armin Schwarz. They both came home in the points too, with Eriksson fourth and Schwarz sixth. Schwarz delivered the Lancer's first podium with third place on the Acropolis, while Eriksson ended the season on a high with second place on the RAC.

However, Mitsubishi was spreading its resources across the WRC programme and its Paris–Dakar project, the Pajero (Shogun). As a result it lacked the funding of its rivals. So despite the potential of the car, with its 16-valve, transversely-mounted inline four-cylinder engine mated to a six-speed gearbox, it was destined to be a bit-part player on the world stage.

Schwarz and Eriksson stayed on for 1994, buoyed by the prospect of the Evo II, which was due to come on stream for the Acropolis. Featuring much improved aero, particularly a neat Gurney flap on the rear wing and a re-sculpted air dam at the front, on paper the new Evo II appeared to be a much more competitive proposition. The suspension had been heavily revised too, with the addition of Ohlins dampers. There were also plans to introduce active diffs, but these proved troublesome to develop and were temporarily shelved.

Schwarz was an encouraging second on its debut in Greece, which he backed up with another podium and third place in New Zealand.

Despite this Mitsubishi was a long way short of the standards its rivals were setting at the time.

The Evo II carried over into the opening part of 1995, and its first win duly followed as Eriksson led home Tommi Makinen for a Lancer 1-2 in Sweden. Ironically this was also its final event, as the Evo III was ready to make its bow on the Tour de Corse.

This time the active diffs – front and rear – were ready, and with Mitsubishi's long-stroke engine ideally suited to the new, smaller turbo restrictors, plus the addition of a larger new intercooler, this meant that by general consensus the Lancer now had the most powerful engine in the WRC. An even bigger rear wing was the final addition to what would be the last of the fourth generation Lancer rally cars.

Andrea Aghini put it on the podium first time out in Corsica, while the first win came two rallies later with Eriksson triumphing in Australia. A combination of accidents and poor reliability prevented the Lancer from holding a candle to the Impreza over the remaining rounds, but it was clear that for the first time Mitsubishi had become a serious player in the WRC.

With the next generation of Lancer not due on line until late 1996, the Evo III was retained for another season, and Makinen shot out of the blocks, recording back-to-back wins on the Monte and Rally Sweden. He suffered engine failure in Indonesia and was second to McRae on the Acropolis, but was back to winning ways in Argentina, which he turned into a hat-trick of wins with victory on the 1000 Lakes and in Australia. He crashed out in San Remo, but

ABOVE Makkinen won four straight titles for Mitsubishi from 1996 to 1999. This is the 1996 car in action in Finland. *(LAT)*

ABOVE Kankkunen used the Celica to claim his fourth world title, in 1993. *(LAT)*

by then he'd already sealed Mitsubishi's first drivers' championship.

Mitsubishi decided against building the Evo IV to the new World Rally Car regulations in 1997, and instead was given concessions by the FIA to make the car to Group A specification. In fact it wouldn't produce a WRC version of the Lancer until 2001, by which time Makinen had wrapped up four successive titles and the Lancer had established itself among the all-time great rally cars.

Toyota Celica GT-Four

Toyota's rallying history on the world stage goes back to the early 1970s, when the Corolla Levin TE27 was entered in a number of events by Toyota Team Europe (TTE), including the 1975 1000 Lakes, which it won in the hands of Hannu Mikkola.

The Celica range didn't become Toyota's competition car of choice until it had reached its third generation, which was launched in 1981. A turbo version came on line in September the following year, and this would become the basis of its Group B contender – the TwinCam Turbo, or TCT for short.

This made its debut on the 1983 1000 Lakes. But despite Audi's Quattro having shown by now that four-wheel drive was the way forward, the TCT was homologated in rear-wheel drive only. However, that didn't stop it from being a winner, and it took six victories during its competitive career, which spanned 1983–86. However, all of these came on either the Safari or the Ivory Coast Rally, events which only counted for the drivers' championship, not the manufacturers', so were often ignored by the works teams.

With no obvious model to convert to Group A spec in 1987, a Supra was entered by TTE on a couple of rallies in 1987, taking third place on the Safari with Lars-Erik Torph at the wheel. However, a new, fourth generation of the Celica model was waiting in the wings, and the four-wheel-drive, turbocharged GT-Four was being prepared to take part in the 1988 season.

With an hydraulic centre diff and six-speed XTrac transmission, double-plate clutch and a transversely-mounted inline four-cylinder engine, the T165 GT-Four was a state-of-the-art machine – and that, unfortunately, meant it was initially unreliable.

It first appeared on the 1988 Tour de Corse, with two cars entered for defending World Champion Juha Kankkunen and rising Swedish star Kenneth Eriksson. Eriksson took sixth, while engine failure accounted for Kankkunen. Veteran Bjorn Waldegaard – the first-ever World Rally Champion in 1979 – joined Kankkunen for the T165's next outing in the Acropolis. Both retired with transmission failure.

Eriksson was back for the Celica's next event, the 1000 Lakes. Again there were engine and transmission problems. The Swede managed another sixth place in San Remo, while Waldegaard registered the Celica's first top three finish with third on the RAC.

Eriksson started 1989 with a third place on Rally Sweden, while Kankkunen finally managed to get to the finish as he took fifth place on the Monte. One of his teammates on that event was a young Spaniard by the name of Carlos Sainz. Four rounds later and the double Spanish Rally Champion had claimed the first of his 97 WRC podiums. The second and third came in his next two outings, at San Remo and the RAC.

Kankkunen claimed the Celica's first win as he led Eriksson home in Australia, but by now he'd become disillusioned with the Celica's lack of reliability and had signed up to rejoin Lancia for the following year. This turned out to be a bit of an error by the veteran Finn, and the Celica had the longevity to match its pace in 1990. Four wins – in the Acropolis, the 1000 Lakes (the first win for a non-Nordic driver), New Zealand and the finale at the RAC – earned Sainz the world title, breaking Lancia's stranglehold on the Group A era.

Sainz took four more wins in 1991, but a huge crash in Australia hurt his chances of defending his title. Alongside him Armin Schwarz scored the only WRC win of his career when he picked up the pieces as an electrical fault forced Sainz out of the Rally Catalunya.

The fifth generation of Celica, the T180, had been introduced as a road car in 1989, but the rally version (T185) wouldn't be available until the 1992 season. Taking full advantage of the lessons learned with the previous car, the Celica Turbo 4WD had significantly bigger air intakes to combat the cooling issues with which it had previously struggled. To improve the car's handling the suspension was completely revised. However, a new hydraulic centre diff proved troublesome, and it was only when it was changed to a viscous version that the car really started to come on song.

The T185 also featured a clever two-way catalytic converter that was tuned to reduce the back-pressure to the turbo. However, it would be another modification to the turbo that would get Toyota into hot water...

Expectations remained high when it made its debut at the start of 1992. However, Lancia's new Delta caught everyone on the hop and Didier Auriol and Kankkunen strode away to victory on the opening two rounds.

Sainz got his challenge back on track with his first and only win on the Safari. A second win followed in Australia, but with Auriol setting a new record for wins in a season the title seemed out of reach. Nevertheless, victory in Spain with Auriol back in sixth created a sliver of hope, and when the Frenchman retired on Rally GB a remarkable title fightback was possible if he could take the victory. He did just that, and

Toyota branded 440 GT-Four ST185s in his name in honour of his achievement.

A clash between his personal sponsor Repsol and Toyota's new main backer Castrol caused Sainz to leave the team for 1993, with Auriol and Kankkunen heading over from Lancia to replace him. It was a disastrous move for Sainz, but manna for the other two. Auriol won first time out in Monte, but with five more wins it was Kankkunen who took the drivers' title. Their combined score – and that of Mats Jonsson, who repeated his feat from 1992 and won the Swedish Rally in a GT-Four – was enough for Toyota to clinch its first manufacturers' title.

It was Auriol's turn to celebrate in 1994, as three wins earned him his first world title. Kankkunen won in Portugal and Ian Duncan on the Safari to ensure that Toyota defended its manufacturers' crown. Towards the end of the season, at the San Remo Rally, a new model was introduced, the GT-Four ST205.

Auriol scored the ST205's only win, on the Tour de Corse, as he set about defending his title. But during routine checks on the Rally Catalunya an FIA scruntineer noticed something unusual in the Celica's air intake on the turbo. After closer scrutiny it was clear that Toyota had been able to circumvent the restrictor, allowing more air into the turbo.

While there was no suggestion that any of the drivers were aware, it was a clear breach of the regulations. Toyota was thrown out of the championship and banned from competing in the WRC for 12 months, drawing its participation in the Group A era to an ignominious close.

BELOW Auriol finally won the championship with Toyota in 1994. *(LAT)*

Impreza Group A results

1993			
1000 Lakes, August 27–29	2nd	Ari Vatanen/Bruno Berglund	L555BAT
	dnf	Markku Alen/Ilkka Kivimaki	L555STE
RAC, November 21–24	5th	Ari Vatanen/Bruno Berglund	L555STE
	dnf	Colin McRae/Derek Ringer	L555BAT
Stage wins	Vatanen:	16	
	McRae:	8	

1994			
Monte Carlo, January 22–27	3rd	Carlos Sainz/Luis Moya	L555REP
	10th	Colin McRae/Derek Ringer	L555SRT
Portugal, March 1–4	4th	Carlos Sainz/Luis Moya	L555STE
	dnf	Colin McRae/Derek Ringer	L555BAT
Tour de Corse, May 5–7	2nd	Carlos Sainz/Luis Moya	L555REP
	dnf	Colin McRae/Derek Ringer	L555BAT
Acropolis, May 29–31	1st	Carlos Sainz/Luis Moya	L555REP
	exc	Colin McRae/Derek Ringer	L555BAT
Argentina, June 30–July 2	2nd	Carlos Sainz/Luis Moya	L555REP
	dnf	Colin McRae/Derek Ringer	L555BAT
New Zealand, July 29–31	1st	Colin McRae/Derek Ringer	L555BAT
	dnf	Carlos Sainz/Luis Moya	L555REP
	dnf	'Possum' Bourne/Tony Sircombe	L555STE
	dnf	Richard Burns/Robert Reid	L555SRT
1000 Lakes, August 26–28	3rd	Carlos Sainz/Luis Moya	L555REP
San Remo, October 9–12	2nd	Carlos Sainz/Luis Moya	L555REP
	5th	Colin McRae/Derek Ringer	L555BAT
RAC, November 20–23	1st	Colin McRae/Derek Ringer	L555BAT
	dnf	Carlos Sainz/Luis Moya	L555REP
	dnf	Richard Burns/Robert Reid	M555STE
Drivers' championship	2nd	Carlos Sainz/Luis Moya	99
	4th	Colin McRae/Derek Ringer	49
Teams' championship	2nd	140	
Stage wins	Sainz	54	
	McRae	52	

LEFT Where it all began: Vatanen and the Impreza on the 1993 1000 Lakes. *(LAT)*

BELOW Sainz was the only works Impreza on the 1994 1000 Lakes. *(Prodrive)*

Monte Carlo, January 21–26	1st	Carlos Sainz/Luis Moya	L555REP
	8th	Pierro Liatti/Alex Alessandrini	M555STE
	dnf	Colin McRae/Derek Ringer	L555BAT
Sweden, February 10–12	dnf	Colin McRae/Derek Ringer	L555BAT
	dnf	Carlos Sainz/Luis Moya	L555REP
	dnf	Mat Jonsson/Johnny Johansson	M555STE
Portugal, March 8–10	1st	Carlos Sainz/Luis Moya	L555REP
	3rd	Colin McRae/Derek Ringer	L555BAT
	7th	Richard Burns/Robert Reid	M555STE
Tour de Corse, May 3–5	4th	Carlos Sainz/Luis Moya	L555REP
	5th	Colin McRae/Derek Ringer	L555BAT
	6th	Pierro Liatti/Alex Alessandrini	M555STE
New Zealand, July 27–30	1st	Colin McRae/Derek Ringer	L555BAT
	7th	'Possum' Bourne/Tony Sircombe	M555STE
	dnf	Richard Burns/Robert Reid	L555REP
Australia, September 15–18	2nd	Colin McRae/Derek Ringer	L555BAT
	dnf	Carlos Sainz/Luis Moya	L555REP
	dnf	'Possum' Bourne/Tony Sircombe	M555STE
Spain, October 23–25	1st	Carlos Sainz/Luis Moya	L555REP
	2nd	Colin McRae/Derek Ringer	L555BAT
	3rd	Pierro Liatti/Alex Alessandrini	M555STE
RAC, November 19–22	1st	Colin McRae/Derek Ringer	L555BAT
	2nd	Carlos Sainz/Luis Moya	L555REP
	3rd	Richard Burns/Robert Reid	M555STE

Drivers' championship	1st	McRae	90
	2nd	Sainz	85
	8th	Liatti	21
	9th	Burns	16
	14th	Bourne	4

Teams' championship	1st	350

Stage wins	McRae	47
	Sainz	31
	Liatti	1

LEFT McRae's win on the 1995 New Zealand Rally was one of his best. *(Prodrive)*

1996

Sweden, February 9–11	3rd	Colin McRae/Derek Ringer	N1WRC
	5th	Kenneth Eriksson/Staffan Parmander	N555WRC
	10th	Didier Auriol/Bernard Occelli	N555BAT
	12th	Pierro Liatti/Mario Ferfoglia	M555SRT
Safari, April 5–7	2nd	Kenneth Eriksson/Staffan Parmander	N555WRC
	4th	Colin McRae/Derek Ringer	N1WRC
	5th	Pierro Liatti/Mario Ferfoglia	M555STE
Indonesia, May 10–12	2nd	Pierro Liatti/Fabrizia Pons	L555SRT
	dnf	Colin McRae/Derek Ringer	N1WRC
	dnf	Kenneth Eriksson/Staffan Parmander	N555WRC
Acropolis, June 2–4	1st	Colin McRae/Derek Ringer	N1WRC
	4th	Pierro Liatti/Fabrizia Pons	N555SRT
	5th	Kenneth Eriksson/Staffan Parmander	N555WRC
Argentina, July 4–6	3rd	Kenneth Eriksson/Staffan Parmander	N555WRC
	7th	Pierro Liatti/Fabrizia Pons	N555BAT
	dnf	Colin McRae/Derek Ringer	N1WRC
1000 Lakes, August 23–26	5th	Kenneth Eriksson/Staffan Parmander	N555WRC
	dnf	Colin McRae/Derek Ringer	N1WRC
Australia, September 15–18	2nd	Kenneth Eriksson/Staffan Parmander	N555WRC
	4th	Colin McRae/Derek Ringer	N1WRC
	7th	Pierro Liatti/Fabrizia Pons	N555BAT
San Remo, October 13–16	1st	Colin McRae/Derek Ringer	N1WRC
	5th	Kenneth Eriksson/Staffan Parmander	N555WRC
	dnf	Pierro Liatti/Fabrizia Pons	N555BAT
Spain, November 4–6	1st	Colin McRae/Derek Ringer	N1WRC
	2nd	Pierro Liatti/Fabrizia Pons	N555BAT
	7th	Kenneth Eriksson/Staffan Parmander	N555WRC

Drivers' championship	2nd	McRae	92
	4th	Eriksson	78
	5th	Liatti	56
	25th	Auriol	4 (just 1 was for Subaru)

Teams' championship	1st	401

Stage wins	McRae	46
	Liatti	21
	Eriksson	10

RIGHT Eriksson in action during the 1996 San Remo Rally. *(Prodrive)*

Index